WITH

D0291604

"All the benefits of serious therapy in one book! Reading this book is like getting therapy from a top-notch therapist who has the guts to tell it like it is and the compassion to help you face your issues squarely and do something about them."

—AMY WOOD, PsyD, author of *Life Your Way*

"Whether you're working with a good therapist, on your own or in a study group, *Living the Life You Love* is a wonderful guide to self-transformation. Paula Renaye's style is easy and comfortable, like a friend who's cheering you on, supportive but firm, as she guides you on the path of self-discovery. I highly recommend this book to those who are serious about transforming their lives."

—MIMI LUPIN, MA, LPC, LSSP, founder of
Making the World a Better Place Foundation

"Paula has written the quintessential manual for anyone who no longer wants to be a member of what I call 'the ain't it awful club.' This is the ticket to transformation for anyone who wants to transcend the fear and negativity that swirls around us and defy the fate of the 'Debbie Downers' of the world. This book will help you dare to confront your angst, claim your heartfelt personal success in your bones and go after it with passion. It will dynamite out those villainous beliefs and paradigms that have been holding you back and let you finally take flight!"

—GAIL MCMEEKIN, LICSW, bestselling author of
The 12 Secrets of Highly Successful Women

"The difference in living a life you love, one you just like or one you really regret is all just a matter of choice. Paula has offered up the perfect menu for living the life that you LOVE, and this book will be one of the best investments in your happiness you will ever make. You owe it to yourself to be your best. Do it!"

—KAREN MAYFIELD, bestselling author of *Wake Up Women*

"The author uses terrific real-world examples to make her points. For those of us wanting something better and don't know how to get there, [this] would be an excellent first step."

—Robin Cain, *Scottsdale Examiner*

"Paula Renaye challenges readers to face what's been holding them back, then provides practical self-discovery tools to move forward. If you're willing to do the work, this book lays out a path for rapid personal transformation."

—Ron Chapman, MSW, author of *Seeing True*

"From the front cover to the back cover, I knew that this book was going to be different than every other self-help book I've read…and I was right! You can't help but be affected and moved by the mirror Paula puts in front of your face. And one of the most wonderful aspects is how she shares from her own life and draws the reader into believing that change, permanent, positive change, is possible. Change takes courage, determination and direction and this book is a blueprint for making those changes in your life!"

—Deidre Hughey, speaker and author of
I Am Bound and Determined

"Everyone or anyone thinking about changing so that they can achieve the life that they want will benefit from this book. Empowerment practitioners, coaches and mentors as well as men and women—the young and mature—thinking about self-development would benefit from the knowledge and wisdom shared. It is a great resource."

—Dr. Cheryl V. Cottle,
founder of CPC Women in Business

"The highest calling we can have as human beings is to honor our hearts. This book is much-needed tough love for courageous transformation."

—Karen Barnett-Bozeman, LCSW

LIVING *the* LIFE YOU LOVE

The No-Nonsense Guide to Total Transformation

LIVING *the* LIFE YOU LOVE

PAULA RENAYE

DIOMO BOOKS

For information, address:

Diomo Books
P.O. Box 21485
Hot Springs, AR 71903
E-mail: info@diomobooks.com
www.diomobooks.com
www.paularenaye.com

For foreign and translation rights, contact Nigel J. Yorwerth.
E-mail: nigel@publishingcoaches.com.

Distributed in North America by
SCB Distributors
15608 South New Century Dr., Gardena, CA 90248
www.scbdistributors.com
info@scbdistributors.com

Library of Congress Control Number: 2012941122

ISBN: 978-0-9674786-9-2

10 9 8 7 6 5 4 3 2 1

Cover design: Nita Ybarra
Interior design: Alan Barnett Design

For
Leah, Mitchell, Layna

CONTENTS

PREFACE

Before you dive into the heart of *Living the Life You Love*, I have some no-nonsense suggestions regarding the people in your life you're closest to—your family and friends.

Those who genuinely care about you want you to be happy, they really do, but sometimes they don't know how to give you what you need when you're not. They may not always know the "right" or "best" things to say when you're going through a tough time or when you're trying to figure out what changes you need to make in your life. Sometimes, they may even want you *not to change* for their own reasons. Just the idea that you want things to be different can make them feel unsettled, fearful or even threatened in a "we live the same life, why isn't it good enough anymore?" sort of way. So, be aware and prepare ahead of time.

As you go through this self-discovery and transformation process, you're going to be taking a hard look at your core beliefs—beliefs you probably don't even realize you have. Many of us have some version of the "I'm not good enough" or the "I'm unlovable" belief that we need to work with in one way or another. The problem is that most—okay, probably all—of these potential points of revelation have their roots in your upbringing and your family of origin. Consequently, though you may be thrilled to discover that the "everybody's always out to get me" belief has been holding you back, people whose worldview depends on that belief may not be. So, be very selective about who you discuss things with.

Gently make sure your friends understand you're not asking for their opinions, interpretations, advice, suggestions, solutions or admonitions right now—only their positive support and encouragement.

When you're allowing your own truth to come up, hearing another person's view of it can be confusing, distracting and disempowering. As much as you may want to ask how you should answer a question or say, *"Please tell me what to do"* at times—don't. This is *your* journey and you *will* figure things out!

Coach your friends and family on what feels supportive and empowering to you during this important time. Just listening is great. Give them examples of comments that you would like to hear, such as *"It sounds like you're discovering a lot about yourself"* or *"That's a really interesting way of looking at things"* or *"I'm really glad you're doing this."* These interactions may be a bit awkward at first, but once everyone gets comfortable with it, it will be a relief for you—and them—and it can help everyone not take things personally.

You also need to gently share what *doesn't* work, such as *"You don't really think that… That's not how it was… That's not what she meant… You shouldn't… If I were you, I would…"* or any version of *"I told you so."* It might be a little hard to say at first, but if you're matter-of-fact about it, reassure them it isn't anything personal, and remind them how much you need their support, they'll get on board. If they don't, it's sure better to know what you're up against now rather than later.

As a bonus, by talking about what you need, you'll both get new options for communicating empathy and encouragement. And, who knows, they may see how much you're loving your life and want the same for themselves.

I know you're ready, so let's get to the introduction and give you an idea how all of this is going to work for you!

Paula Renaye

INTRODUCTION

Living the Life You Love. It's what we all want to be doing, isn't it? But how do we get there? How do we find what ignites our passion and makes our hearts sing, and start living *that* life? How do we transform the life we have into one we just can't wait to jump out of bed and enjoy living every day?

Well, that's what this book is all about, giving you a way to find out what your dream life really looks and feels like, why you're not already living it and how you can. It's first and foremost about understanding you—the real you. It's like a true best friend who'll wrap an arm around your shoulders and tell it like it is. A friend who'll tell you what you *need* to hear, not what you want to. Then, with a solid "you can do this" pat on the back, she'll hand you a step-by-step guide to find your own answers—and solutions. It may sting a bit from time to time, but if you'll stay strong and keep digging, the insights you discover will speed your progress faster toward joy than you ever imagined possible.

I offer you this tough-love approach because it worked for me in a way that all the commiserating, sympathy, positive spinning and "let it go" talk never could. I wanted my life to be different and daydreamed about how I wished things were, but nothing ever changed. No matter how happy I said I was—or how loudly I complained that I wasn't—my problems remained.

My in-your-face moment came after I had regaled my longtime best friend with yet another rendition of "poor me." When I finally took a breath, she said to me, "Isn't it great that for the rest of your life, no matter who you tell that story to, they'll say, 'You poor thing.' And you, my friend, can be a victim forever!"

Well, that stopped me in my tracks! But I couldn't get mad about it, because I knew it was true. So, right then and there, I changed my way of thinking—about the situation and about myself. I vowed never to see myself as a victim or tell that story ever again.

It was a huge step, but there were more to be made, and I did not make such stellar progress in other areas of my life. As you will soon see, I kept myself trapped and in pain far longer than even I can believe. Looking back, I wish someone had sat me down, eyeball to eyeball, and said something like this:

Look, I know you're in pain, and I hate seeing you hurt. I've done everything I know to try to help you. I have listened and sympathized. I have offered suggestions and recommendations. I have sent you websites, books, CDs and movies to help get you through this. Nothing is working. So, because I care about you and I care about myself, I am going to tell you that you have to make a choice. You can choose to stay in pain if you want to. It's your life. But if you do, I will assume that your situation and your pain are what you want, and I will honor your right to keep them. I will no longer make suggestions about things you can do to feel better, nor will I suggest that you change anything about your life. I will also no longer listen to you complain about your drama, because it serves no purpose. Either do what you need to do to change what you need to change, or admit that you don't want to and shut up about it.

Ouch. Yes, it would really hurt to have someone say that sort of thing. But it could also be exactly what you need to snap you out of denial and get you moving forward. I'll never know if it would have made a difference for me back then. I hope it will make a difference for you now.

A lot of material is packed into these pages, but you won't find any highbrow theories that sound great when you read them and not so great when you try to put them into practice. What you'll find are simple concepts, including real-world examples, to help you evaluate your own situation, along with practical tools to put them to use. It's a crash course in self-discovery—a way to map where you've been and where you want to go, and to uncover the roadblocks keeping you from getting there.

As you read this book, take what feels good to you and start doing it. Keep working with it as you move on to the next thing that feels appropriate, and continue to add more techniques to your toolbox as you go. What speaks to you one moment may be completely different in the next, so just go with it and trust that you'll get what you need when you need it. Go back through the book as many times as you need to. You'll probably get something different each time, depending on what's going on in your life and what you need most at that point.

Each chapter offers opportunities to identify the chinks in your armor; however, you don't have to go in any particular order to benefit from this book. You can start at the end and work your way backward. Or you can just randomly open the book and see if there's something inspiring for you in that particular section at that particular time. Make it easy. Find what works for you and use it.

A word of warning here: This is called the No-Nonsense Guide for a reason. If you don't find something in this book that triggers some important emotional reaction, then you don't need to be reading it! If something you read gets your hackles up or strikes you as completely ludicrous, *celebrate*!

What actually happens when you get that emotional hit is that something you've just read has triggered a limiting belief and you've reacted to it. That's great! Don't fight it. Don't ignore that little cringe of discomfort or twinge of anger. Write down everything that comes to mind, such as *"There is no way that's right because . . ."* or *"That's the dumbest thing I ever heard; everyone knows . . ."* Embrace every thought, because what comes out in these precious moments can give you more insight into yourself than you ever dreamed possible. You'll also find that the insights will start to snowball on you. You'll like discovering why you do what you do and realizing that you can change it if you want to.

Choosing the no-nonsense, tough-love approach takes courage. It's hard to take that first look in the mirror and not blink, but it's absolutely essential. It's also critical to remember that while this *is* about facing hard truths, it's *not* about beating yourself up over where you are in this moment. We *all* have made plenty of mistakes, and if we had time machines we'd probably go back for some do-overs. But we can't, and keeping our shame and guilt fresh serves no one.

So, take the loving approach for yourself, as well as for those you wish you'd done better by. Do the tough work and move on. Acknowledge the past, accept responsibility for your part in it, then forgive yourself and focus on making better choices now.

This book gives you the tools to do all that and more. They work, and it's my hope that by using them you will find your way much better and faster than I did. I do want to make it perfectly clear that I don't profess to have mastered everything in this book—or that I don't have plenty more to learn. I still get angry. I still behave in reactive ways. And, I still use the techniques in this book to deal with my challenges. Today, however, it doesn't hurt like it did at first. It's fun... most of the time.

At the end of each chapter, you'll find a "Transformation Insight" section where you'll apply the concepts in the chapter to your own situation. Some are short and some are fairly long. All have a purpose, and I encourage you to be tough and make yourself really work with them. Even if you think the answers seem obvious or the questions silly, do it anyway. By taking the time and letting your thoughts—any thoughts—come to the forefront, you can find out what's really calling the shots in your life.

Be sure you have something to record your insights on. You can use the space provided in this book or you can use a separate journal, digital document or whatever works for you. Restaurant napkins, scraps of paper and envelope backs are less desirable, but do whatever it takes. The process of writing it down is important—do it!

Okay, it's time to get to work. The sooner you get started, the sooner you'll be living the life you truly love!

CHAPTER 1

WHAT ARE YOU WILLING TO DO?

If you value it, you'll make time for it.
If it's important to you, you'll make it happen.

What are you willing to do to live the life you love? What are you willing to do to get what you *really* want?

These seem like simple questions, don't they? The answers may seem simple too, and you may be thinking, *"I'll do whatever it takes to get what I want,"* or *"I'll do anything, absolutely anything, to fix my problem."* Well, these are nice thoughts, but they aren't true. I know for an absolute fact that you won't do "anything." I won't.

If my goal is to have more money, I'm not willing to rob a bank to get it. Are you? That's an extreme example, but it does highlight the fact that things may not be as clear-cut as you think.

So, let's try it again with a bit of a twist. Are you willing to *change yourself* in order to get what you want and live a life you love?

Talk about getting to the hard stuff right out of the gate! Seriously, think about it. Are you willing to let go of some of your thoughts, beliefs and behaviors? Are you willing to consider that something you thought of as "just the way it is" may not be? Are you willing to change critical aspects of your life to get what you say you want? How much of the way things are right now—the way *you* are right now—are you really willing to change?

I can hear you already: *"Of course I'm willing to change. I know I need to change some things or I wouldn't be reading this!"*

Not so fast.

How about where you live? Are you willing to move? Quit your job? Go back to school? End a relationship? We all *think* we're willing to do anything—absolutely anything—to make things different in our lives in order to accomplish a goal we say we want or to stop some pain that has us on our knees. But is it really true?

Let's try a different question: What in your life are you *not* willing to change? Your job? Where you live? How often you talk to your mother? What you eat? Who you hang out with? Whether you have pets? What you do in your spare time? Who you live with?

Before you can realistically expect your dreams to come true, you have to figure out why they haven't already. Recognizing what you're *not* willing to do is a great first step.

For example, if you have a full-time job and watch television four hours every night, and you're not willing to quit working or stop watching television, then it's going to be difficult for you to meet a variety of goals. You can't go back to school unless you take weekend classes. You can't work out every other day unless you park an exercise machine in front of the television.

I Want to Do That

When people learn that I'm an author and have written a number of books in both fiction and nonfiction, they often share their own desires to write a novel or their life story. I always encourage them, but I also recognize that few will actually ever do it. Why? Because they really don't want to. They like the *idea* of writing a book—and there's a part of them that wants to—but the reality of doing it is something entirely different. Writing is a lot of work and there are simply other things that are more important—at least at the moment. It's a fact, because if they *really* wanted to write a book, they'd already be doing it. They'd be sitting in front of their computers writing instead of staring at the TV, shopping, playing golf, volunteering or whatever currently takes up their leisure time.

It all comes down to priorities and choice, and it's true for every situation. There's really only one reason we don't do things: We don't want to—other things are more important.

If you value it, you'll make time for it.

If it's important to you, you'll make it happen.

If you really want to, you will.

So, here's the deal: If you say you want to make a career change, but you need more education or a particular certification, then stop talking about it and put your time and energy toward figuring out how to make it happen. If you keep complaining about how unhappy you are in your relationship, figure out what it's going to take to make you happy and get to it. The bottom line is if what you're doing now hasn't gotten you what you say you want, *something* has to change. If you want something different than you have right now, you absolutely, positively *must do* something different.

Either do what you keep saying you want to or quit saying it. Whether it's to lose weight, get another job, move, eat better, be less critical and judgmental, exercise more, get a divorce or whatever, you need to either do it or simply admit that you don't want to and stop putting it out there as if you do.

Saying it without doing it may keep it as a possibility in your mind, but what it's actually doing is reinforcing that the conscious "me" can't be trusted—it's just talk. So, when words like "I want to do that" slip out of your mouth, get clear in your own head what you really mean. Maybe you really do want to do it, but haven't yet. Or, maybe you admire the skill, talent and effort it takes, and would admire yourself if you had that accomplishment.

Whatever the case, be honest with yourself. It may seem like an inconsequential thing to do, but every time you come clean with yourself and speak truth in one area, you take a step closer to owning all your truths.

Now, here's your first Transformation Insight opportunity, which is designed to help you find the parameters that you have to work with. Once you know what you're *not* willing to do, it's easier to see what choices you *are* willing to make and how those can move you toward your goals.

Remember, it is essential that you do these Transformation Insight exercises in *written* form. Use your workbook, journal, notebook, paper or electronic document and write whatever comes to mind.

TRANSFORMATION INSIGHT 1

List five things you are *not* willing to change or give up.

1.

2.

3.

4.

5.

Don't panic. Just write down whatever came into your mind when you read the statement. Be honest about it, even if it's something you would rather not admit. You aren't being graded and you don't have to do anything with the list. These are just notes of your thoughts at a particular moment, nothing more. Some options are: where you live, where you work, career or education goals, living alone, who you're married to, what you do on the weekends or evenings, decisions related to family and children, personal independence, identity, financial considerations—anything that is important to you.

CHAPTER 2

THE WHY

It isn't what you want or don't want, or what you do or don't do, that's revealing—it's the why behind it.

In Chapter 1, you identified five things that you don't want to change in your life, which is great! You've started thinking about your true priorities and now have a list of factors and considerations to work with as you define your goals and identify steps to achieve them. You've also opened the door to realizing what you *are* willing to do, but we'll get back to that later. First, we need to do a little more digging and get some even more important information.

Many times, it isn't what you want or don't want, or what you do or don't do, that's revealing—it's the *why* behind it.

Too Stupid to Live

In my life, the one area that was off limits to change was my relationship. I couldn't imagine *not* being married. So, I tolerated the intolerable. It took a long time to realize what I was doing, and longer still to figure out why. Eventually, I discovered I had a belief system, ingrained from birth, that tied my identity and worth to having a man in my life.

Consciously, I was an outspoken teenager with the "I am woman, hear me roar" attitude of the times. I couldn't wait to get out of high school. *I* had a plan. I'd figured out how I could fast-track my degree and my career, and in no time I'd be my own boss, walking into my high-rise CEO office in a designer business suit and barking out orders. No one was going to tell me what to do, not at work and not in my personal life. And I didn't care what anyone said, I wasn't having kids. I thought any woman who had children was an idiot, and if she gave up a career and stayed home with them, well, she was just too stupid to live.

Oh, yes, I said that—repeatedly. Granted, I was a know-it-all teenager, but I believed it was true, and it was how I intended to live my life. However, what I said consciously that I would never do, and the subconscious programming in charge of what I was *actually going to do*, were working with two vastly different scripts.

Of course, you know where this story is going. In spite of all my bold talk, I did exactly what I said I wouldn't in every way, shape and form. I walked away from a promising journalism career because working late at the university newspaper upset my new husband. I quit school to support him in his career, and eventually I became a "too stupid to live" full-time stay-at-home mom.

Now, my kids are great, and I am really proud of them. I'm also deeply grateful that I had the opportunity to stay home with them when they were young. At the time, however, I wasn't fully on board with the being grateful thing. Some days, I felt smugly superior because I was at home with my children while all those heartless career women were missing out. Other days, I felt like a failure. I felt unworthy of breathing the same air as "successful" women. I wanted so badly to be someone other than Mommy and the maid. I wanted to be someone who accomplished things and who was acknowledged for her intelligence, talents and abilities. I wanted the me back that I'd lost, but I didn't want to give up what I had. I both loved and hated my life, and my brain couldn't reconcile the two. My conflicting beliefs about career, marriage, motherhood and choice only added to my downward spiral.

So, why did I do it? Why did I do exactly what I said I would never do? Why did I become the very person I said I despised?

The Prime Directive

As it turned out, while my conscious self was busy making plans for a life that explored my highest potential, my subconscious programming was lurking in the background with a nasty little monkey wrench. In my case, it was a prime directive that trumped everything else. "Be all you can be" did not dictate my priorities and choices—"be married or die" did.

I could say anything I wanted to, but if it didn't fit with my deeply held belief that without a man to validate me I was nothing, it wasn't going to happen. It couldn't. My self-worth—my worthiness to even be alive—depended on having a man, so I did whatever I had to in order to accomplish that. I gave up my education, my career, my dreams and my identity.

Besides having to get married as soon as possible, which I did at eighteen, my programming also required that I *stay* married, no matter what. And I did—for decades. Only when the mental, emotional and physical pain became more than I could bear did I become willing to *begin* to admit that I was seriously unhappy with my marriage and my life. And only when the reality of staying married became more painful than the fear of dying if I wasn't did I finally become willing to consider a change.

However, recognizing that I wanted things to be different didn't instantly fix things. My husband made it very clear that *I* was the one with the problem. *He* hadn't changed, I had; therefore, all the issues in the marriage were entirely on my shoulders and it was up to me to deal with them. He was right. Maybe not in the way he meant it, but right nonetheless. He *was* still the same person, doing the same things he always had. I *was* the one who had changed. I was the one who now didn't like the role I was playing and wanted more. And yes, it *was* up to me to deal with it and make myself happy.

That left me with two options: try to brainwash myself back to where I could tolerate the situation, or do the unthinkable and change it. As it turned out, the very thing that I needed to change to become whole and healthy—get out of the marriage—was the exact same thing my subconscious programming thought would kill me.

Many of us have an ongoing internal conflict between what we think we *should* want and what we really *do* want. Who we *want* to be is very different from who we think we *have* to be. And most of us don't even realize it. We just do what we are driven to do and then try to make it okay. We don't really know *why* we do what we do.

Have you ever thought about why you make the choices you do? Are you making those choices deliberately and on purpose or just because? Are you being who you want to be or who you think you have to be? Are you doing what you really want to or what you think you should?

Before you can figure out what *you* truly want, you must first determine the "whys" behind what you do and want now. As you saw above, having to be married was the why behind just about every choice I made. So, what's one of your whys? Is it related to self-worth? Is it about fear of not having enough? Of being less than? Being unloved? Alone?

After exploring your *whys*, you may have realized you have a few more things you'd like to add to your "not willing" list. Great! We all have extenuating circumstances (other people, children or other important factors) that affect our decisions, and those have to be taken into consideration. The purpose of this book is not to create an inflexible set of absolutes. It's about expanding your awareness so that you can see your situation as realistically as possible and make conscious choices accordingly.

The Belief Monkey

It can get pretty intense when you're looking at your limiting beliefs and subconscious programming. So, sometimes, I like to think of that part of me that's behind the scenes calling the shots as a thing—a Belief Monkey. I imagine an impish face, sitting at a control panel, constantly scanning the world and matching it with my subconscious belief system, then pushing the programmed button on what I do about it.

It took me a long time to realize I had beliefs I wasn't consciously aware of. Now I am always on the lookout for limiting beliefs that are keeping me stuck in a place I don't want to be. When I find one, I reframe it into an empowering belief and tell my little monkey friend to get busy changing the programming. It can take a time or two, but once I've consciously identified the old thinking, and then turned it into a belief that serves me, it's much easier to stay on track.

I like the Belief Monkey way of looking at things because it puts an active spin on the "monkey mind" approach. Instead of just quieting the monkey mind or detaching from an old script, it's a one-two punch that puts your Belief Monkey to work with a new empowering script to replace the old thought pattern. You don't have to work at overcoming anything—no fighting against—just switching around. Much easier!

Already on the Fast Track

Can you feel it? Are you already zooming ahead, thinking of how to put this concept to work for you? I hope so, because it's simple, it's easy to remember and it works—fast. This isn't the last you'll see of the Belief Monkey either. He pops up throughout the book to show you how to put the technique into practice.

Now that you've taken a monkey off your back and put him on your side—so to speak—I bet you're ready to get to this chapter's Transformational Insight exercise. You've zoomed through a lot of questions and thought-provoking statements, which have already jumpstarted you to see ways to track down your own limiting beliefs. Do it. Be fearless even when it gets uncomfortable—especially then. Don't hold back on anything. If a thought comes up, write it down. The thoughts you don't want to admit are the ones you need to most. So, no matter how silly or horrible it may seem, write it down. Your notes are for your eyes only, so have the courage to be brutally honest with yourself. Once you confront your truth, you'll be amazed how much easier it will be the next time. Soon enough, you'll be looking for your own ways to dig deeper and find out even more about yourself.

Remember, your *only* goal for this process is to come out the other side a happier, more fulfilled and more joyous you. Be willing to allow *that* into your life and the rest will take care of itself.

TRANSFORMATION INSIGHT

1. Review your list from Transformation Insight #1 of the things you are not willing to change. Add those to the "What" column in the table below.

2. In the second column, write down why you are not willing to change or give up each thing on your list. A simple example would be "I'm not willing to change where I live because I love my home and the area. My family is here and it is important for me to be close to my family."

3. In the third column, note a belief or fear that might be influencing your choice. Beliefs can support the choice or be the reason for it. To continue the example above, your belief might be "Family comes first" or "You have to sacrifice for love." You get the idea.

Remember, there are no wrong answers—only insights. Write as much or as little as you need to, and if something that isn't on the "What" list comes up, explore that too. If a thought came up about it, there's a reason, so go with it.

If you feel anxious about having to explain why you don't want to change or give up something in particular, don't ignore it. Put a laser focus on it and find out what's going on at a deeper level. What you discover will be invaluable.

What	Why	Belief/Fear
1.		
2.		

What	Why	Belief/Fear
3.		
4.		
5.		

CHAPTER 3

JUST LOVE YOURSELF?

Any time I started feeling confused,
anxious or in turmoil over something, I grabbed
respect by the throat and demanded answers.

I gave a talk recently on how to put your transformation on fast forward, and during the question-and-answer period, a man from the audience commented on how much he liked my presentation, but said that none of my suggestions were necessary if you just loved yourself. I understood what he meant, but I'm not sure he did. The more he talked, the clearer it became that he liked the *idea* of loving yourself, but didn't really know what to do with the concept in his own life. As with all of us, saying the words was one thing—living them was quite another.

Twisted Thinking

My mother used the "love yourself" phrase on me when I was growing up, presumably whenever what I'd done had seriously undershot the mark. But no matter how many times she said it, I never understood how loving myself would have fixed things. Besides, it seemed like pointless advice anyway. Didn't we all love ourselves by default?

A good friend gave me the best explanation I've ever heard. He said it was treating yourself the way you would treat the person you cared about most in the whole world. I like that. In practice, however, the transference thing proved cumbersome for me. Having to stop and decide if what I was about to do would be appropriate for someone else before I did it for myself was beyond my abilities—or at least my patience. Besides, if I did that, wouldn't it make me selfish, self-absorbed, narcissistic, egotistical, vain or greedy?

The answer was no, and I understood why, but I still couldn't make the concept work. That one little four-letter word—love—kept tripping me up. It has so many different meanings and nuances, varying with the situation and the person interpreting it, that it's tough to pin down. "I love this pie" has a different level of emotion and meaning than "I love my husband," or so one would presume. But maybe not. And dare we even mention adding the word "unconditional" into the mix?

Now, I realize the title of this book is *Living the Life You Love*, and what I'm saying may seem contradictory, but it really isn't. It's easy for me to grasp loving my life, particularly because I know what it means and how it feels when I'm not loving it—that, I get. Granted, I've had plenty of moments when I hated myself, but that still didn't make the "love yourself" concept work in my head. Then again, how could it, given my programming and beliefs? In my world, "love" was something you could only *get* from someone else and could only *give* by giving up your sense of self. Try to plug those meanings into *love yourself* and make it work. Exactly, you can't.

A Respectable Option

Given the programming I had to work with, "love yourself" was not a motivating factor for me. Unfortunately, I didn't have anything that made any better sense. Then one day I started noticing the words I used when I talked about my marriage and the rebound relationship that came after it. I heard myself saying things like *"If I'd had a shred of self-respect I never would have done what I did."*

That's when the lightbulb came on. Respect! I could wrap my mind around *that*. Love might have myriad meanings, but respect was clear-cut in my mind. There was no worry about slipping into selfishness or egotistical behavior either, because respect didn't have those kinds of connections. It worked for me—and had been working for a while. I just hadn't understood what I'd been doing until I finally heard myself say it enough times.

With my new awareness, I realized I could start using respect on purpose. The first thing I did was take a brutal inventory of how I hadn't respected myself in my life. It was neither brief nor pleasant. In fact, it was horrible to admit what I'd done and allowed. But it was necessary. Once I realized how I'd stripped myself of self-respect, I knew what I had to do—and not do—to get it back.

To keep myself straight on that, I made respect my mantra. I ran it in my head like a ticker tape, whispered it like a prayer and shouted it as a vow. And, yes, I also spelled it out in song and dared the world to find out what it meant to me. Any time I started feeling confused, anxious or in turmoil over something, I grabbed respect by the throat and demanded answers.

I started looking myself in the mirror and asking: *Would a person with high self-esteem and self-respect do what I'm doing? Consider what I'm considering? Think what I'm thinking? Tolerate what I'm tolerating?*

And then, I asked myself an even more important question—*why?* Why would someone who respected herself do that? Why wouldn't she?

Knowing *why* what you're doing is respectful to yourself—or why it isn't—is critical. By having the courage to answer that one little question, you'll get amazing insights into what's really going on in the situation—and in your subconscious programming. If you'll let yourself dig down to the bottom layer of truth, you'll know what serves you and what doesn't—and what you need to do about it.

There's one more question that will also help keep you pointed toward happiness. It's simple too, and pretty obvious, but it's important to consider and it opens the door for even more insights: *Does this get me closer to what I really want?* Again, after you have your yes or no answer, dig in to the why of it.

As you work with these questions, you'll begin to see things you haven't been able to before. New thoughts and insights will come up—let them. Even if they make you cringe or feel like you've been punched in the gut, honor—and write down—every thought and feeling. The ones you don't want to face are the very ones you must. Your job is to get clear on the way things are, not the way you pretend they are.

Remember, just because you recognize reality and admit the truth about a situation doesn't mean you have to turn your life upside down this very minute because of it. The only thing you have to do right now is gather information.

TRANSFORMATION INSIGHT

Think about a situation where you felt in turmoil, where you felt stuck or tied up in knots and didn't know what to do. Use the top section of the form below and describe what was going on. Then, below that, list the choices you had. For each of those choices, answer the following questions:

1. Would a person with high self-esteem and self-respect do this? Why or why not?

2. Does this get me closer to my goal? Does it get me closer to what I really want? Why or why not?

For instance, if you were facing a challenge at work, you might describe a situation where you were being asked to do something you didn't feel good about for one reason or another. List all the choices for dealing with the situation. For each, decide if it's something a person with self-respect would do and then explain why. And then you have to decide if it gets you closer to your goal. Now, as we know, this is a tricky question and you have to be clear on what you really want. If you want to keep your job at any cost, your answer may be different than if your goal is to work in an environment where you are happy and fulfilled.

Start with a situation you've already experienced and know the outcomes your choice created so you get a feel for how it works. Then, try it on a situation you're facing right now.

Describe situation:

Choice considered	Self-respect?	Why or why not?	Closer to goal?	Why or why not?
1.	☐ Yes ☐ No		☐ Yes ☐ No	
2.	☐ Yes ☐ No		☐ Yes ☐ No	
3.	☐ Yes ☐ No		☐ Yes ☐ No	

Use these questions and this template as a filter—a litmus test of sorts—any time you feel unsure about making a particular decision, catch yourself in a mental loop of faulty thinking or find yourself in a situation that's causing you pain. Try it on anything!

CHAPTER 4

CARROTS AND STICKS

---

*Sometimes, until we're forced, we stay right where
we are, tolerating what we know we need to change
and making excuses for why we can't.*

Some days we really do need a cheerleader, someone to motivate and inspire us, to tell us that we can do it and to believe in us no matter what. We all need carrots! At other times, all the cheery support in the world won't get us to do what we know we need to. On those days, it takes a stick to get us moving.

Yes, like it or not, sometimes the only reason we take action is simply to avoid the pain it will cause if we don't. We'll stay stuck until it hurts more *not* to do something than to just face it and get it over with.

For example, I do not enjoy grocery shopping and will find all kinds of ways to avoid it for as long as possible. However, when I no longer have any kind of decent food in the house, the scales tip and I haul myself to the grocery store. I will do what I really don't want to do (shop) in order to avoid something I like even less (starving).

That's a very simplistic example, but you get the point, and it applies on the emotional side of things as well. Take relationships—romantic, parent-child, friend, work, and so on. If you're in turmoil over it, you know something needs to change, but what's going to make you actually do something about it?

That's right, it has to hurt enough. You will take action only when the pain and heartache of keeping the relationship as it is becomes greater than your fear of not having it at all. Until then, you—like me—will make extended excursions down the River of Denial, paddling along with your best friend Delusion, trying to talk yourself out of your feelings while you pretend all is right with the world.

After my twenty-five-year marriage ended, I leaped immediately into another relationship with a man I affectionately call Rebound Guy. Oh, I was in love—at least in the high-flying infatuation and chemistry sense of the word—no question about that. However, in spite of that—or maybe because of it—the things that had been wrong in my marriage were now wildly wrong in that relationship. It was a roller-coaster ride that took me to the highest of highs and sent me plummeting to the lowest of lows, with jerks, twists and stomach-flipping loops in between. My life never felt smooth—there was no even keel. I was either schoolgirl giddy or deeply depressed.

I did everything I could think of to make things work—at least in my head. I walked on eggshells, turned myself into a human pretzel and spent countless hours trying to guess at what was actually going on with him and the relationship. I was sure that *I* was the problem, because whenever he explained why what he'd done shouldn't make me feel bad, it always sounded so logical and I felt silly and ashamed for even mentioning it. Clearly, I was just not seeing things right, and if only I could, then everything would be okay.

The Bad List

Convinced I wasn't being fair to Rebound Guy, I made a list of all the good and bad things he'd done. The idea behind the exercise was to remember and focus on the good and ignore the bad, which is exactly what I dutifully did. I memorized my list and clung like a drowning rat to the few good and marginally good things I'd written on a single sheet of paper—and valiantly ignored the three-ring binder full of things that had cut me to my core. Ignoring the bad stuff—the clear evidence that things were seriously wrong in the relationship—did not fix things. It only widened my disconnect with reality, supported my delusions and kept me stuck and miserable.

Eventually, when I began to allow myself to see the truth of my situation, I had to stop focusing on the few positive aspects of the relationship because they just confused me. I had to take the opposite approach. I made a condensed version of the Bad List and kept it with me at all times. When I hurt or felt myself getting sucked back into delusion, I focused on that list, remembering the pain of each event and reminding myself that I deserved better.

My internal programming was hard to convince, and I still went back to him—more than once. However, things were changing for me even though I didn't realize how or why. By making and using that list, I'd forced myself to see reality and had started honoring the idea that I deserved better. The Bad List was my stick, and, unbeknownst to me, it was helping me reclaim my self-respect.

Same Game, Different Ending

As I gritted my teeth and pushed my way through the temptations, I began to feel better. I started feeling confident and empowered, and I liked it—I liked me. Those new good feelings were a big, huge carrot and I wanted more. The stronger I became, the easier it was to recognize the traps before I stepped into them. At the first hint of the old patterns and pain, my red flags went up. It became harder and harder to rationalize, justify or excuse his behavior, and one day I just didn't.

When my moment of truth came, we were playing the same game we always had—my questioning his behavior and him explaining why I had no reason to. But something was different—I was different. I heard my voice repeat the familiar tired lines of the same worn-out script, but it didn't feel the same—the old emotions weren't there. I wasn't terrified or tied up in knots or walking on eggshells to say the right words. My life no longer depended on the outcome of that conversation. Something inside me had changed, and I knew I would never play that game again.

In the end, I didn't explain or announce my decision, I just stopped saying my lines, said goodbye and hung up. As I watched myself end the call, I knew I had just reclaimed my power, my life and myself—I had witnessed my own transformation.

Self-Help Math

You too can make the carrot and stick work for you. Since we know that we'll often do more to avoid pain than to go for the good stuff, use that tendency. Focus on the bad stuff and put yourself in as much pain as possible so you'll be willing to go for the carrot and get out of the situation quicker.

In the grocery-store example at the start of this chapter, I confessed that I generally won't go shopping unless I'm forced—the starving stick gets me moving. But if I really wanted to always have good food in the house, how could I motivate myself to do *that*? What's a different stick I could use and what might be a motivating carrot?

Well, the first time I went to look for something healthy and tasty and didn't find it, I wouldn't just make do. I'd focus on how much I wasn't going to enjoy eating whatever I could scrape together and how it would make me feel sluggish, bloated and yucky (stick). Then I would jump to how good it would taste—and how I'd feel later—to have great food that I enjoyed available whenever I wanted it (carrot). I put myself in more pain first then gave myself a way out.

Here's a little self-help math to explain things a bit further.

The Stick
Denial + Delusion = Pain

The bottom line for the stick is this. If you keep ignoring reality and continue to create delusions so you can live in denial, your pain *will* get worse. There's no way around it. Granted, you may get the illusion of relief in the short term, but when reality pops up again— and it will—the dial on the pain meter will ratchet up another notch too. And, at some point, one of two things will happen. You'll either reach your personal threshold for pain tolerance and snap like a twig, or you'll give up and become sad and bitter, blaming others and perpetually complaining to anyone who'll listen.

So, use the stick to your advantage. Keep reminding yourself how much it hurts to keep doing what you're doing. Feel the pain. Don't try to ignore it, suppress it or distract yourself with something else. Feel it so you'll deal with it.

The Carrot
Reality + Self-Respect + Action = Joy

Going for a juicy carrot seems simple enough; however, when you've been living in the land of denial, using delusion to avoid reality, it can be a tough leap to imagine living every day in joy. Sure, you might be able to wish and daydream in generic terms, but that's just part of the fantasyland coping program you're using to tolerate what you know you need to change. You aren't actually going to do anything about those dreams—you can't, because you're not dealing with reality.

Wishful thinking and airy-fairy hoping aren't real carrots—there's no active motivation or incentive to do anything except continue to wish and hope. So, if your current version of happy is tolerating and making do, you must tend to that first. You have to get clear on where you are (reality) before you can get moving (action) to where you want to be (joy). And the key to that is self-respect.

Since people with self-respect won't tolerate situations that cause them pain, use that to your advantage. When you look at things through the lens of self-respect, you'll get a very clear view of what you *don't* want, which is the stick part of the equation. However, the process also opens the door for seeing the flip side of that picture—what you really *do* want. Wishes and hopes turn into real-world carrots, and you'll find yourself chomping at the bit to have them.

Using the stick and the carrot together is a powerful way to fast-forward your transformation. Instead of looking for ways to keep from feeling bad about something that's wrong in your life, make yourself feel *really* bad. Don't wait until you reach your break point—create it. Ditch the denial and delusion nonsense, face up to reality, and take charge of your life and your happiness.

It's actually easier than you might think, and this chapter's Transformation Insight gives you a powerful two-step shortcut out of misery and into joy—take it! When you make friends with reality, respect yourself and act accordingly, you'll be amazed how good you feel and you'll wonder why you didn't do it sooner. You'll also be amazed how much time and energy you'll have for fun and happiness when you aren't spending it trying to avoid pain or finding a way to tolerate and pretend you're happy about it. In your new reality, you won't need a spin doctor to make things *seem* okay, because you'll truly be loving your life and it will be more than okay—it will be great!

Sound too good to be true? It isn't. You just have to be willing to do what it takes to get there. So, let's find some of your own carrots and sticks and get to it!

Think of a situation that is causing you pain of some kind. (If you need ideas, go back to your situation in Transformation Insight 3 where you determined how your choices were self-respecting and moved you toward your goal—or not.)

Make a list of all the good and bad aspects of the situation. (The philosophy that there are no "bad" experiences is a "good" one, but it isn't going to help us here, so just go with it!) After you identify each point, explain why it's important to you, why you want to keep it in your life—or why you don't.

Describe situation:

Good points	Why you want or don't
1.	
2.	
3.	
4.	
5.	

Bad points	Why you want or don't
1.	
2.	
3.	
4.	
5.	

Now, use the following questions to explore more aspects of your situation.

1. What are you doing about the situation now that's not working?

2. What do you need to do but don't want to?

3. Why don't you want to?

4. What would motivate you to take action?

5. Is that a carrot or stick? Something you want—or want to avoid? Explain why.

6. How can you use it to motivate you to action?

Use this process for as many situations and options as you need to.

CHAPTER 5

WHAT'S BEHIND THE MASK?

*The best way to live a sad, lonely life is to
spend it trying to please someone else.*

Let's talk about masks. We all have them. There's one for strangers, for a first date, when we're feeling insecure, and for a job interview, and there are some for parents and children, just to name a few. We've all created façades to hide behind at one time or another. Often, we wear temporary masks to get through difficult situations we don't feel strong enough to tackle otherwise.

Sparkle!

I remember years ago when I was speaking at a conference in Tucson. It was the one and only time my husband and children had attended an event with me, and it was not working out well at all. My husband was incredibly uncomfortable, maybe embarrassed even, with me in the spotlight. Needless to say, his discomfort, and its ripple effect on the kids, wasn't helping me be my usual perky self.

Before the panel, one of the authors, whom I knew from other events, noticed I was a little "off." As we walked into the room, she told me that before Shirley Temple performed, her mother always said, "Sparkle, Shirley, sparkle." Then, my friend put her fingers to her cheeks, cocked her head from side-to-side and mimicked the famous child actor as she chirped, "Sparkle, Paula, sparkle." I couldn't help but laugh, and I was back to my smiling self when we started the program. With just a few words, she helped me put on my "author" mask and do what I needed to do. The panel went great, we had everyone laughing and I had a great time. To this day, I still say those words to myself whenever I need to "sparkle."

So, even though we think of a mask as something we hide behind, it isn't automatically a bad thing. My Author Mask helped me set aside the emotional turmoil of my personal life and tend to my business. It helped me bring out an authentic part of myself—my author-speaker self—that might have been difficult for me to access otherwise in that situation. It didn't make my problems go away; it just kept me from taking them on stage with me. Being able to slip on that mask kept me from dragging my career down with my relationship woes—at least at that moment.

Fake It 'Til You Make It

Another mask that comes in handy is the one you put on to act "as if." You mentally become the person you would be if your goals were already a reality. You become your future successful self today.

The As-If Mask is tried and true, but it's not about pretending that you're someone you're not or that you know something you don't. This mask is about finding the confidence within yourself to step up and not be intimidated by situations, people or success. It helps you stand tall and walk shoulder to shoulder with those who might otherwise make you feel like an insignificant amoeba in an ocean of successful whales.

We've all seen someone nervously explain that he's never done this sort of thing before and basically beg not to be judged for the mistakes he's sure he's about to make. It's painful! Instead, put on your As-If Mask and act like you've done it a thousand times before. Don't pre-apologize or make excuses, just do it! And whatever happens, handle it as a pro who has done it a thousand times.

That applies to any situation—business, school, hobbies, social situations and even personal relationships. Don't put on a fake persona, just be the real, authentic you—the version without all the worries, fears and insecurities. And the good thing about using this mask is that eventually you really do become more confident and self-assured. You fake it until the real you shines through automatically.

Cover-Ups

An important distinction of the Sparkle and As-If Masks is that they are used to bring out an authentic part of self—not to create a fake personality to hide behind or use for manipulation. If you're using a mask to pretend to be someone you're not, or you're hiding behind denial and delusion to avoid confronting a necessary truth, it's a problem—big one.

And here's the even bigger problem—it's usually not just a one-time thing. Just as the As-If Mask can help you become confident in yourself, a cover-up mask becomes a habit as well, but not in a good way. Wearing that kind of mask suppresses your authentic self. You slip behind an invented character and become *less* real—you become a caricature of yourself.

My Sparkle Mask served me well. The one I put on afterward didn't. The Pretend-Nothing's-Wrong Mask helped me avoid facing the reality of my unhappy situation—it made things *seem* not to hurt as much in the moment. However, allowing myself that fleeting wisp of relief meant I couldn't do anything to rock the boat, such as go for my goals or admit that I wanted to be living a different life. Wearing that mask trapped me in a self-defeating cycle of tolerating what I knew I needed to change and pretending I was happy about it.

Who we become and why fascinates me, and I've known quite a few people well enough to get a glimpse behind their masks. Given my programming, it's no surprise that I've spent a lot of time trying to figure out men. Since our society doesn't appreciate males showing emotions, it stands to reason that most of them were exceptionally good at hiding their true thoughts and feelings, which made getting a good "read" on them tough and effective communication even tougher. I had to learn the hard way that a blank face on Man A did not automatically mean the same thing it did on Man B. The same look on one face might mean, "Yes, I hear what you're saying and it is agreeable to me," and on another it might be silently screaming, "How dare you not tell me what I want to hear! I hate you!"

One man I knew appeared to be easy-going and happy, laughing about anything. After I got to know him better, I realized it was just a persona he had developed. He was never *not* wearing a mask of some kind. His words and actions were calculated, making it difficult to tell which were genuine and which came with an agenda. He took great pride in being able to conceal his true thoughts and bragged about using his "raccoon mask" to control situations, particularly with his boss and his wife. There was a time when he came close to admitting that the only person he was hiding from was himself, but, ultimately, it was just too scary and too painful. He slipped the mask back on, bolted it in place and returned to the safe and familiar.

Another man could appear cool, calm and totally unaffected in situations that had my heart racing just hearing about them. He'd face whatever it was and never flinch, twitch or even blink. I had great admiration for the skill, and it served him well in many cases—he'd be the guy you'd want beside you in a crisis. But it also came with a price, particularly in personal and business relationships. Because people couldn't get a good read on what was going on behind the mask, it made developing trusting relationships difficult. If something triggered the old fears and patterns from childhood, he went into survival mode and did whatever was necessary to make those old feelings go away. His actions often left others totally confused by the experience and created an escalating cycle of distrust.

Other men wore the Arrogant Bully Mask to cover the sensitive feelings of an insecure child who never felt worthy. The little boy in the adult body had to use bluster, boasting, bravado and bullying to feel good about himself. If you've ever worked for an autocratic, authoritarian dictator, you can relate. Bullies and dictators will do whatever it takes to shore up their fragile egos. They'll criticize and attack whoever or whatever didn't go their way, and they'll lie and blame-game until they've rearranged reality to their own liking—at least in their own heads.

There are many types of masks, and while these last examples are of men, the same principles also apply to women. We *all* have masks and protective devices, and we all developed them in the same way for the same reason—as defense or coping mechanisms.

Family Ties and Reality Lies

We each grew up in a family and environment that provided us with a particular set of behaviors, situations and circumstances and we each adapted accordingly. In loving and nurturing environments, what we learned helped us thrive. In more challenging circumstances, what we learned may have helped us simply survive.

Children who grew up in unsafe circumstances—physically, mentally or emotionally—had to learn ways to adapt and protect themselves. Some learned to keep a blank face and pretend they didn't hurt. Others endured by becoming invisible. Some developed particular personas to ingratiate, distract or deflect. Others found creative ways to avoid pain by outsmarting and manipulating. All learned to lie in one way or another. Unfortunately, the skills that helped them survive as children are the very ones that cause them the most trouble as adults.

We all have a story—a history of experiences—and we all have masks and protective devices we've cultivated because of it. We all know that, and a part of us wants to look unflinchingly in the mirror and face the truth about ourselves. Another part, however, instinctively knows that doing so will bring us to our knees. With a lifetime of protecting against the pain, it can be very difficult to be willing to put away the mask and expose old wounds. We feel naked and vulnerable, as if we're facing the old pain all over again—as if we're staring death in the face.

That's how it feels. That's not how it is.

As you've already read, facing my own reality pulled the rug out from under me and turned my world upside down. It seemed like everything I'd believed to be true about my life and myself wasn't. The masks I'd hidden behind had shattered before my eyes, and no matter what I did, I couldn't put the pieces back together. I felt betrayed, abandoned and more alone than I ever had in my life. I felt like I was going to die. Sometimes, I wished I would. Because the dragon I knew I had to slay to save myself was the very same one I was certain I would die without.

As I worked through my own process, I discovered a lot of things about myself. During my separation and divorce phase, I moved from Colorado to Missouri, where my aunt lived. She had always been like a second mother to me, and with the passing of my mom three years before, she was also my last living close relative other than my children. Since she too was dying, I wanted to be with her to help her through her transition—and I wanted her to help me through mine. In the few short months we had together, she told me more about the family I had grown up in than I had learned in all the years prior. Her revelations were not happy ones, and it was difficult to hear her admit the truth of the life she'd lived behind her own smiling and stalwart mask. More difficult yet was realizing how I had lived behind that same mask myself.

I don't recall much of my childhood, but one memory that seemed insignificant turned out not to be. I was about six years old. My mom had picked me up from the babysitter after work, and instead of going home, we'd gone to my aunt and uncle's house down the street. They had a big pecan tree in the front yard that I loved to climb. When we got there, however, I forgot about that, because something felt wrong. Everyone was standing out in the yard, acting funny. Then, I saw my dad on the far side of the tree, leaning against it, bent over. He looked really bad and I was terrified. I didn't know what was going on except that he was obviously really sick and no one was helping him. I tried to go to him, but my mom held me back. I cried and begged her to go help him, but she wouldn't. She told me nothing was wrong, that everything was fine and we were going home.

Well, as I discovered many decades later, my instincts had been correct. Things had not been even close to fine. My daddy *had* been very sick, and the reason my mother hadn't rushed to do anything about it was because he had also been very drunk. It was not an uncommon event either. It was, however, a snapshot moment that explained a lot about why I thought and behaved as I did. I had learned, just as my mother and everyone else in the family had, to put on my Pretend-Nothing's-Wrong Mask and go on. I learned to "not see."

A defining moment of just how good I was at that came in the therapist's office. She asked me if I'd heard of Al-Anon. I thought it was an odd thing to ask, but I said sure, and moved on to something more important. When she brought it up again, I asked why. She told me that some of the things I said—and the way I said them—were typical of someone who had grown up in an alcoholic family. I was shocked that she would suggest such a thing and I told her in a big hurry that there most certainly had not been any . . .

As the words left my mouth, the truth rushed in—and the mask came off. Just about every male on my mother's side of a very large family had been an alcoholic, including my father, of course. And, as my aunt's confessions had revealed, alcoholism had been only the tip of a very unpleasant iceberg that included a variety of disturbing addictions and predilections.

It was horribly unpleasant to have to face the truth—and allow it to fill in what my mind had blocked. But once I did, those fuzzy memories came into focus and things started to make more sense—*I* started to make more sense. Yes, the picture was ugly, but seeing it was also a huge relief. I wasn't crazy! There wasn't anything inherently wrong with my eyesight, my feelings or my instincts. In fact, they had always been right on. What was wrong was what I'd been trained to do about them.

"Not seeing" had been an essential coping—and even survival—skill for me as a child. As an adult, however, it was the very thing that caused me the most trouble. Once I took off the Pretend-Nothing's-Wrong Mask—once I was willing to see the truth—I could heal from it. I didn't have to remember every terrible thing from my childhood—I still remember very little—but knowing the truth helped me move past it and stop repeating it in the present.

My story isn't a new one—alcoholism, addiction, abuse and codependency issues are well documented. But until I was pushed, I couldn't see it—I wouldn't see it. So, please, if anything here rings even the tiniest of bells, get the help you need and break the old patterns. You'll be so glad you did!

Get a Clue

So, how do we recognize these old patterns? How do we make ourselves see what we have never seen? How do we know when we're hiding behind a mask? How do we find our truth?

The first thing to do is so simple that you'll want to ignore it—don't. Start paying attention to your thoughts, feelings, words and actions. Yes, it's that simple—and that important.

I spent a lifetime trying to rationalize away that inner voice that was telling me things weren't right. I used faulty thinking to explain away my feelings and do what I thought I was supposed to. What I felt, said and did were always at war, and it kept me in some state of turmoil most of the time. I felt distracted, disjointed, disconnected and disgusted, not to mention scattered, scared and sick.

So, there's a great clue—your body. If what you're thinking, feeling, saying and doing don't match, you probably feel it physically. A headache, churning stomach and stiff neck are a few ways your body tells you things aren't right.

Think about how you feel when you say or do something that isn't in line with what you really think or feel. What happens? Does your jaw tighten, stomach churn, face twitch, heart race? From now on, when you notice a reaction in your body, stop and take inventory. Is what you're feeling or thinking the same as what you're saying and doing? Why not? Start with what you actually said or did and work backwards.

A simple example is when someone asks you to do something that you don't want to do. What's your first reaction? How does it make you feel? Do you automatically say no? Do you make up excuses? Do you feel obligated to say yes? Do you feel resentful and grumble inside, but put on your Pretend-It's-Okay Mask, smile and do it anyway? How do you feel when you go ahead and do what you didn't want to? Or, if you tell them no, how do you feel about that?

Asking yourself these kinds of questions—and answering them honestly—gives you wonderful opportunities for self-discovery. Taking each question to a deeper level by asking why will uncover even more insights into your thought processes and why you do what you do. Take the time and do it!

Many of us have spent our lives trying to be who we thought we should. We put on our masks to cope and survive. We stuffed down what we truly wanted and twisted ourselves into who we thought "they" wanted us to be. We were afraid not to. If we allowed ourselves to be who *we* wanted, the message was clear: no one would ever love us and we'd live sad, lonely lives. We felt we had to conform or be abandoned.

The truth is that the best way to live a sad, lonely life is to spend it trying to please someone else. So, stop trying. Start figuring out what masks you've been wearing—and why—and start letting the real you come out. It may be uncomfortable at first, but stick with it. You may be surprised at how great your authentic self is and how much *you* like *you*!

For this Transformation Insight, we're going to start with figuring out how your thoughts, feelings words and actions line up. And since we've touched on some pretty deep stuff here, I want to emphasize again how important it is to take care of yourself and do what is best for you. So . . .

If You Need Help, Get It

Now, by this point in the book, you may be thinking there are people in your life who need a lot more help than you do. That may be true— probably is—but it isn't your place to say so. It's fine to look at other situations and learn from analyzing them. It's not okay to try to come up with solutions for others. You can make a suggestion and offer a reminder, but anything beyond that is just plain nagging.

I tried to get my husband to go to counseling. I begged, I pleaded and I nagged, but he emphatically refused. He made it quite clear that I was the one with the problems, not him. So, I did the only thing I could do—I agreed. I had a problem and I went to get help for it. And I allowed him to choose not to.

If your partner, spouse, family or friends do choose to share the journey with you, it can be incredibly empowering and healing for everyone. It's why when one person goes to counseling, the rest of the family is encouraged to go too. A positive change in one person can spur positive changes in whole families. When people learn new ways of looking at situations, managing their emotions and communicating their thoughts more clearly, the group starts interacting differently and more effectively.

A specially trained counselor or therapist can help individuals understand why they do what they do and make positive changes, but they also focus on the interactions of the family. Ideally, while the individual heals, the family dynamic transforms as well, becoming more supportive and positive for everyone.

If you realize you need or want professional help—and a lot of us do—find a qualified counselor or therapist who specializes in the outcomes you're looking for. It isn't a life sentence; it's just another tool to get your transformation moving quicker. I had a wonderful counselor when I first moved to Arkansas. She made it crystal clear from the beginning that we wouldn't be dragging this out for years; this was a "get in, get the work done and get out" program. I loved the approach, obviously, since it is the same one I advocate here.

The differences between types of counselors can be significant, however, so finding one that works for you is key. Finding particular certifications, such as Marriage and Family Therapists (MFTs), can be helpful for focusing on relationship dynamics and such. If mental illness is a possibility, a clinical psychologist or psychiatrist might be more appropriate. My counselor was a Licensed Clinical Social Worker (LCSW), and she was just who I needed. She helped me immensely and quickly, and I recommend her highly, so a personal recommendation is a good place to start as well. The fit has to be right for you—and it's up to you. Do your homework and trust your instincts.

People give all kinds of reasons and excuses for not getting help. Shame, embarrassment and pride can be factors, but it generally comes down to fear. It can be terrifying to face things you've spent a lifetime trying to avoid, and it may seem easier to just keep running from it—it isn't.

So, again, if you need help with this process, I strongly encourage you to get it. Therapists and counselors tell me they recommend this book to their clients to help speed up the therapeutic process—the book supports the therapy. The reverse is true as well—counseling can support progress in this book. Whatever point you are on your journey, get what you need so you can start living the life you love *now*!

TRANSFORMATION INSIGHT 5

The first part of this exercise explores the thoughts, feelings, words and actions you had in a particular situation, how well they were in agreement and how your body responded because of it. You'll also play out how you felt toward the situation, yourself and others afterward—and how it might have been different.

In the second part of the exercise, you'll get a template for looking at the masks you wear and how their positive and negative attributes and effects are at work in your life.

1. Describe a situation when you did something you didn't want to do because you didn't have the courage to say no.

2. What were your first thoughts when asked? What did you say?

3. How did your body respond? (Chest tight, groan, cringe, grit teeth, etc.)

4. How did it feel when you said yes when you didn't want to? Why?

5. How did you feel when you did what was asked?

6. Afterward, how did you feel about the person? About yourself?

7. Explain how your thoughts, words, feelings and actions were in alignment—
or how they weren't.

8. How do you wish you had handled the situation?

9. What kept you from handling it that way? What was the fear?

Now that you've identified how you responded and felt when you did
something you didn't really want to, let's look at another situation where you
might automatically slip on a mask. Some examples include: when you're at
work, church, club meetings, restaurants or public events, visiting people in
hospitals, with a spouse/parent/child, on a date or a job interview, interacting
with someone you don't like, being around someone you have a crush on.

For that situation, explain the limitations your mask imposes, such as a Happy-Face Mask you wear in the office to hide your anger and disillusionment with your boss or a First-Date Mask so you don't say anything stupid.

Go into detail about the positive and negative aspects of the mask: Does it keep you focused? Does it help you feel courageous or empowered? Help you be your best? Protect you so you won't be criticized? How might wearing the mask be deceptive, manipulative or harmful? Do you dress, talk or act a particular way so someone will like you? Do you pretend to like football or ballet because you know the other person does?

Go into as much detail as possible—the more you dig, the more you'll find!

Mask name:

1. Describe the situation where you wear a mask.

2. How does the mask limit your words or actions?

3. Describe the positive aspects of the mask.

4. Describe how using the mask protects you.

5. Describe how using the mask deceives or manipulates.

6. Describe how using the mask is harmful to you and others.

CHAPTER 6

RIP OFF THE BANDAGE

Until we realize it's actually more painful to keep the hurt hidden than to tear off the bandage, clean out the debris and let the wound heal, we'll keep avoiding it.

Okay, you've gotten a look at some of your dragons, you've agreed to take off the mask and you've started realizing how your thoughts, feelings, words and actions need to be on the same page. You've also faced the fact that there could be pain involved in this process. So, you ask, how bad is it going to hurt? The short answer is—a whole lot less than if you don't face it.

What They Don't Know Can't Hurt Me

Think of it this way. A little girl falls down and scrapes her knee. There's dirt in the wound and maybe even some gravel. It hurts and she cries, but if she tells her mother, she'll have to endure having the wound cleaned and doused with medicine, which will hurt even more. So, she dries her tears and sticks a bandage over the scrape to hide it—what Mom doesn't know can't hurt her. She goes back to playing and forgets about it for a little while.

Every now and then, she bumps it and it hurts, but it's not nearly as bad as how she thinks it will feel to have it dressed properly, so she ignores it. Before long, however, there's some yucky yellow goo oozing out from under the bandage and it's really sore. She still has the same problem, though—it'll hurt more if she asks for help. Now, however, there's another problem too. If she *does* decide to let her mom fix the wound, the bandage has to be ripped off first, and that's even more pain. Deciding that if she just gives it a little more time, the goo will go away and it will quit hurting on its own, she grabs more bandages and gets to work, hiding and protecting.

We've all done this sort of thing in one way or another, and we keep doing it, until we realize that it's actually more painful to keep the hurt hidden than to tear off the bandage, clean out the debris and let the wound heal.

It can take a long time to be willing to rip off your protective layers and expose your pain. Yes, it is going to hurt a little at first—maybe a lot. Growth sometimes does. Just as physical growth can be painful, a rapid expansion in self-awareness can be uncomfortable, too. As with many things, however, the fear of pain is ultimately worse than the pain itself.

The dread of jumping into a cold swimming pool on a hot summer day is worse than just doing it and getting it over with. We all know that, yet some of us still have to creep in slowly and let ourselves adjust, little by little. That's okay, too. Just make a commitment and dip a toe in the water—gently pick at the edge of the bandage—and it will happen. You'll soon find that exposing and healing your wounds is much easier than you thought it would be. You can even have fun with it. Here's how I did.

Reroute the Crazy Train

My personality is such that when I latch onto a plan, I'm like a bulldog with a bone. I gnaw at it until I chew up every shred. Some might want to put a pesky clinical label on it, such as obsessive-compulsive, but my answer to that is—it's not *always* a bad thing.

I used to spend a lot of time analyzing my partner and his possible motivations. I spent countless hours trying to figure out what he might be up to so I could potentially manipulate the outcome or mitigate the fallout. The rationalizing, justifying and excusing was hard work. It was also a fool's errand, and spinning my wheels on that project didn't get me anything except a ride on the crazy train.

Still, there was merit in practicing the process—the analysis, focus, dedication and determination. Yes, some might call it obsessive, but that's the point. If we work with what we have, we can turn a negative into a positive. If you're going to obsess, wouldn't it be better to focus your energy on healing the wound rather than hiding from it or pretending it's okay when it isn't? You're going to expend the same amount of effort either way, so you might as well use your own idiosyncrasies to your advantage.

Initially, I focused my laser attention on my role in the relationship problems, analyzing what I'd done wrong and why and how I could have done it differently. While it's essential to take responsibility for your actions and choices, I took things a step further and made all the problems in the relationship solely my fault. No matter what he did, I ignored it and looked only at my part in the situation.

Now, that sounds like the correct approach—to focus only on your own role because you can't change anyone else—and it is. Unfortunately, I wasn't seeing the whole picture—or the other half of the problem. I convinced myself that if I could just become more aware, more evolved, more mature or whatever, then I wouldn't feel bad— what *he* was doing would make sense to me. Nothing would actually change, but I'd be enlightened and the relationship would magically transform accordingly. Consequently, I excused behavior that didn't need excusing. What I was doing made as much sense as the little girl with the scraped knee trying to figure out how she could change herself so the rocks wouldn't be rocks anymore.

Once I realized that, I started shifting my focus from changing me to save the relationship to changing me to be happy and healthy— regardless of who was or wasn't in my life. I rerouted the Crazy Train in a healthy direction—I became obsessive about getting free of the old patterns and beliefs that had kept me stuck in a situation that made me miserable.

So, instead of trying to suppress your particular personality traits and quirks, find a healthy and productive way to use them to get what you really want. Get in there and start uncovering and cleaning out your old wounds. Take responsibility for your choices and actions, but don't take responsibility for others. Pay attention to the whole picture. Let yourself see reality and then deal with it. This journey is about facing your pain head on, healing it and coming out the other side healthier and happier than you've ever been.

You've already got your finger poised on the edge of the bandage—I know you do. Now, go ahead. Rip it off and let's go!

In this exercise, think of an old issue you know you need to deal with but haven't. Come clean with yourself on why you haven't. If you're afraid that seeing the truth would mean you'd have to deal with it and that would mean your life would have to change, then admit it—and be specific with the hows. Explore what it's costing you to keep avoiding the issue. Go into as much detail as possible. Uncover every pain point and feel it as you work through the questions. Then, after you're very clear on the price of keeping your wound, go just as deep into the benefits of being free of it—the feeling of weight lifted, the release of stress or relief of pain in your body, feelings of joy.

1. Identify one wound/issue that you've ignored.

2. Describe the pain you might have to face (e.g., rejection, criticism) if you took off your protective bandages and let yourself see the wound. What are you afraid might happen?

3. What is the likelihood of your fears coming true if you face the issue?

4. What is the likelihood of your fears coming true anyway?

5. What pain are you living with because you haven't dealt with the issue?

6. What's the cost—what do you give up, miss or lose because you don't resolve the issue?

7. What limitations does it create in your life?

8. If you faced the old wound, what stress would be relieved?
   How would it bring feelings of relief?

9. What could you do then that you can't do now?

10. In what ways would your life be better because you dealt with this old wound
    once and for all?

CHAPTER 7

FOLLOW THE
YELLOW BRICK ROAD

---

*We all fear change to one degree or another, and our particular
quirks show up in what we say and do and how we see the world.*

We've already seen fear in action, but now, it's time to get down to the
nitty-gritty specifics. We don't like to admit it, but we all have fears.
Some of us are pretty good at pretending we don't, but they're still
there and they always catch up with us—always.

In *The Wizard of Oz*, the Wicked Witch terrified Dorothy at every
turn in ways she didn't see coming. Dorothy couldn't hide from her
fears and neither can you. You too have to journey down the yellow
brick road to get to know yourself, face your fears and figure out that,
in the end, you don't need a wizard or anybody else because you can
very well save yourself. We all know that, and it sounds obvious and
easy, but it's not so easy when you're the one having to do it.

Our fears can take many forms. Mine may be, and probably are,
very different from yours. What you might not give a second thought
to might absolutely terrify me, and vice versa. One fear isn't worse than
another. There are no silly fears and no silly or embarrassing reactions
to them; they're just markers on the road of life that we've collected.

We all came by our phobias in unique ways, and we can get past
them in our own ways—if we want to. That's really the only require-

ment on this journey—you have to want to take the trip. If you want to be free of your fears and limiting beliefs, you can be, but you have to be willing to make the effort. Understanding why you have the fear in the first place is a good start.

Flying Monkeys and Jumping Spiders

Actually, I'm going to talk about spiders, but the flying monkeys always scared me too, maybe as much as the Wicked Witch. In fact, as a kid, watching *The Wizard of Oz* was a pretty terrifying experience. It's what inspired my Belief Monkey analogy. Those flying monkeys—those fears and unconscious programs—will swoop down and sweep you up before you know what hit you and whisk you off to the creepy castle to be tortured by the evil witch as the soldiers chant and sand slips out of the hourglass. I'm probably over all that—probably—but even if I'm not, I'm not going to take the time to deal with it right now.

Quite frankly, a lot of fears just aren't worth the bother. I have a highly developed fear of spiders. When I was about two years old, some kind of spider bit me near my eye and I almost died. I don't know if it was a venomous spider, an allergic reaction or what, I just know it put the fear in my family. Consequently, everyone who loved me tried to keep me away from spiders, and the belief that "spiders will kill me" became embedded in my subconscious as well as my conscious awareness.

Now, generally, I can overcome the programming enough to capture one in a container and return it to the wild—unless it jumps at me, or even worse, leaps out of the container. Then, all bets are off. The most likely outcome in that scenario is that I will simultaneously scream, jump, drop the container and flee in the opposite direction of the spider. Eventually, I will get control of myself, laugh nervously and get back to the business of finding and catching the thing, which will be way harder at that point, because I'll be shaking like a leaf, having barely escaped certain death.

I consciously know it's silly, but that's my Belief Monkey in action.

I'm not proud of it, but since I don't have to deal with spiders often, I am not motivated to spend much time changing it. Since I don't care if I am totally free of that fear and the subconscious limiting belief, I would have a hard time working on letting go of it. I just don't *care* enough. Consequently, I'll probably never be calm and peaceful catching spiders, and I am okay with that.

Refusing to face a debilitating fear or belief that is negatively impacting your life and happiness is another matter entirely. Only you know which category applies and whether you care enough to make changes.

It's Only Paint

About four years ago, I bought my condo and did significant renovations. Unsure what I wanted to do for color, I painted it all a basic cream, figuring I would take one room at a time and add color. I did and have continued to do so—repeatedly. A few months ago, I painted most of the rooms again. My master bath is on color number six, the kitchen is on five, and the living and dining room are now a fourth color, unless you count the two accent walls I added last month.

Now, you may think that's crazy, and for some people it is. For me, however, my inner and outer worlds both reflect and influence each other, so the paint is just a part of my ongoing personal evolution. I'm not the same person I was when I moved in here—or even three months ago. When I birth a new inner version of me, I like to upgrade my outer world accordingly as a way of paying tribute to the changes that aren't visible with ones that are.

It is worth noting that some of us will use anything—including painting and decorating—as our drug of choice to avoid dealing with the internal voice that's telling us we need to make other changes in our lives. That's a different thing, and we all have to determine the truth of our own situations and self-police accordingly.

We all fear change to one degree or another, and our particular quirks show up in what we say and do and how we see the world— what we're willing to do and what we're not, and yes, even how we feel about painting the walls.

I have a friend who has recently begun to see how her fears have seriously limited her life. She'd moved into her home about ten years ago, but hadn't done a thing to the place since. Her walls were stark white and her furniture and decorations were from her mother's estate, right down to the crocheted doilies on the tables and the old family portraits in every room. Honestly, it was like walking into my grand-mother's house—and she died thirty years ago. Granted, it could have been simply a style preference, but it wasn't. It was fear.

Her fears showed up in everything she said and did. She viewed the world through the lens of "what could go wrong." I once joked that she should get a job as an actuary because she could identify the worst possible scenario for anything. It kept her from doing a lot of things. If she did decide to do something, she made extensive preparations to guard against all the "what ifs" her mind created. Suggesting she think of "what could go right" and how much fun it would be didn't help. She was determined to see the world as a scary and dangerous place.

It was fascinating to observe, but it was a simple comment about paint that gave me an insight into the root of her fears. When I men-tioned that I'd bought a new color and was working on the living room again, she was a bit shocked. Hadn't I just painted it a few months before? What was wrong with me? I could almost see her head spin-ning through the phone. "Well," she finally said, "what if you don't like this color either?"

Huh? Now, *that* is a crazy question. For me, it isn't even a question at all. It seems obvious that if I don't like it, I'll change it—it's only paint. For her, however, it was a huge risk and it made her uncomfortable even hearing about it. After all, she hadn't changed anything in her life in over a decade. Keeping things the same—and tolerable— was her goal.

As we talked a bit more, I realized she believed that if she made any changes, she'd have to live with them the rest of her life, which, given general life expectancies, was at least thirty to forty years down the road. It was an unconscious mindset that "you only get one shot, so you better not screw it up." She was so afraid of making a mistake that it was better not to try than risk failing. In her mind, I suppose I was a great failure—just look how many "mistakes" I'd made on my walls. There was an unspoken shame associated with it, and somehow my choices seemed to make *her* feel bad. Then I said one little word that rocked her world—*why*.

She eventually began to realize that she had a long list of fears and limiting beliefs that—as with all of us—were programmed from birth. She had learned to just accept things as they were and not want for too much—there was no point since she couldn't ever have it anyway. It was better to do nothing than risk the possibility of pain. If you didn't go swimming, you couldn't drown. If you didn't aim too high, you wouldn't be disappointed. There are many more, of course, but the bottom line was that she had spent her life not really living. She was surviving just fine, but she certainly wasn't enjoying it. How could she be? Her focus was on avoiding pain, so in order to avoid it, she had to constantly be thinking about it—she had to live in fear.

What Makes You Shake?

What are your greatest fears? Can you list five? Ten? Are you afraid of small, dark spaces? Heights? Snakes? Failure? Success? Not being good enough? That someone will see through to the "real" you and realize you're a fraud? Are you afraid to let the real you come out? Afraid of getting older or being old? Losing your hair? Getting sick? Being alone?

Sometimes, maybe most times, we don't consciously know our deepest fears or the limiting beliefs attached to them. We simply react the way we've been programmed to. It is only when the automatic reactions become problems in our lives that we begin to notice. We may complain that the same kind of situation keeps happening over and over—we're constantly being taken advantage of in some way, feeling like victims or not being treated the way we think we should be.

As we saw with my friend above, people who grew up believing that the world was unsafe and that everyone was out to get them will take that with them into adulthood and that reality will be reflected back to them. Those who see the world filled with kind, loving and helpful people will see that reality and be less likely to feel victimized. People who believe that all drivers of red cars speed will look for situations that validate that belief. They'll notice the red sports car zooming past on the opposite side of the road, but the white truck going the same speed behind it won't register. If you're focused on it, you'll find it.

Scarred for Life

Sometimes, our fears aren't even our own. I didn't develop a fear of spiders because I made the connection. I was too young to even know what a spider was, that it had bitten me or that I'd nearly died because of it. My parents and caretakers certainly knew and they wanted to make sure that it never happened again. It wasn't an evil plot to ruin my life or make me look silly as an adult; they were genuinely afraid I'd play with spiders and die. The same is true with my friend's family. They didn't sit down and script out ways they could keep her repressed and fearful. They were just passing on their own fears and limitations and, in their own way, trying to spare her some of the pain they'd experienced.

Even when our intention is to keep the child safe, we can inadvertently instill fears. Here's another example. If you are afraid of water, you could have had an experience as a young child that instilled a deep fear and you may not even consciously remember it. Your parents might not either, but the programming from the event is still there. Maybe as a toddler you figured out how to open the back door and went exploring...

It's a wonderful, sunny day and you're over at a neighbor's house with your mommy, having fun in the backyard. It's fun playing in the sandbox, but then you see some toys over by a big pool of sparkling blue water. You toddle over to take a look and decide to stick your hand into the water. At that very moment, Mommy calls. You look around, smiling, thrilled with your new experience.

But then she screams—a high, piercing screech. You jerk your hand out of the water, terrified. What's wrong? Something bad is going on! You begin to cry. Mommy rushes over, grabs you up and begins to yell and cry, and maybe even swats you. Oh, this is bad! You have done something very bad! Mommy is very mad, and you don't ever want that to happen again!

Not much of a leap to understand why someone might not be interested in swimming or being around water, is it? Again, the mother didn't plan to make the child hate swimming pools; she was just terrified that if her baby took one more step he would die, so she did what came naturally to prevent it.

The Road to Oz

If you have a strong reaction to something, such as water or spiders, there is a past experience somewhere that led to that fear. I don't remember the spider incident, only what I was told about it. You may or may not consciously remember what happened to cause your particular fear, but you can still reprogram it if you want to. Each time I deal with a spider calmly and without incident, it reinforces the knowledge that I will not die from being near one, and my unconscious belief has a little less power. I push myself a bit as well. Even when someone else is around and willing, I do my own spider wrangling.

As with anything, the more you face the issue, the easier it gets. You simply keep doing it until the new pattern is set—the monkey will learn. Affirmations can also be helpful. However, an "I am not afraid" statement is ineffective. It will not overwrite the "I *am* afraid" script. Use a statement such as "I am peaceful and calm around spiders and it is easy for me to deal with them."

This simple example relates to a fear that doesn't impact my life, but the same process of understanding can work with any fear. In many cases, though, figuring out *why* you have the fear is important because it gives you the tools—the understanding of old family patterns and limiting beliefs—that you can use to clear it. Of course, if you have severe phobias, anxieties or panic attacks, you may need to get professional help. As always, you must decide what you want and need.

Just like Dorothy, you have to follow the yellow brick road, face the witch and the flying monkeys, expose the man behind the curtain and use your ruby slippers to get home. I always wondered why she chose the path she did—there were other choices—and I always worried that she had taken the "wrong" one. Well, there is no wrong path, only shorter or longer versions. Because you're reading this right now, you've automatically chosen the shortcut. You've taken personal responsibility for yourself, your life and your choices. That is the most important thing you can do and the quickest way out of the creepy castle.

So, let's break into song and get to skipping!

TRANSFORMATION INSIGHT 7

In this chapter's Transformation Insight, you're going to determine what you think your five greatest fears are right now. You may think of others later, and that's great, just go through the process again at that point.

For each fear you find, note whether you want to get over it and whether you think you can—or not. Then explain why and describe any thoughts or feelings that come up. Be sure to write down any limiting beliefs, uncomfortable feelings or "silly" thoughts. Those silly thoughts and uncomfortable feelings are exactly what you're hoping to find—they're the keys to understanding what's really going on.

Name fear	Do you want to get over it? Do you think you can?	Why or why not? Describe any thoughts or feelings that come up.
1.	Want to? ☐ Yes ☐ No Can you? ☐ Yes ☐ No	
2.	Want to? ☐ Yes ☐ No Can you? ☐ Yes ☐ No	
3.	Want to? ☐ Yes ☐ No Can you? ☐ Yes ☐ No	

Name fear	Do you want to get over it? Do you think you can?	Why or why not? Describe any thoughts or feelings that come up.
4.	Want to? ☐ Yes ☐ No Can you? ☐ Yes ☐ No	
5.	Want to? ☐ Yes ☐ No Can you? ☐ Yes ☐ No	

CHAPTER 8

THE PRINCESS
AND THE REBEL

---

*Once we understand the positive and negative aspects of ourselves—
and the beliefs that fuel them—we can turn them to our advantage.*

The Princess and the Rebel. Sounds like a hot romance novel, doesn't it? The pretty princess, her hair billowing in the breeze, and the rebel rogue ready to sweep her off her feet and whisk her away to his castle. It's the stuff romantic fantasies are made of, right?

Well, this story is more of what happened after the two lovebirds made it to the castle—or, in this case, my head. The Princess and the Rebel (female version) are the two primary archetypes—the two wildly divergent voices in my head and my psyche—that have called the shots for most of my life.

Although most of their antics occurred on the subconscious level, I figure their conversations went something like this:

PRINCESS *(hands clasped at her heart): Oh, I just can't wait for my Prince Charming to rescue me, love me and take care of me forever in our happily ever after.*

REBEL *(hands on hips): Hey, Cupcake, that little scenario sounds like a prison sentence to me. I don't know what you're thinking, but nobody's going to be telling me what to do. Furthermore, anything some man can do, I can do better, just watch me!*

PRINCESS: *You hush that silly talk. You act like that and nobody is going to ever love us.*

My brain jumped back and forth between these viewpoints so fast that it all blurred together into one big tail chasing that even I couldn't keep track of. I had no idea who was talking when, and half the time I didn't even make sense to myself. I can only imagine how it looked from the outside.

We all have this sort of counterproductive programming to one degree or another. What we say and what we do don't match, and they can be mismatched in a variety of ways, depending on which of our unconscious scripts is running at the time. It may look crazy to others, but we are simply following the orders of the belief system that's calling the shots at the time.

Of course, there are positive aspects to these archetypes too. Rebel has served me well in so many ways. I have a long list of "impossible" things I've done thanks to her "just tell me I can't and I'll show you" determination. That's been a double-edged sword, however. While it gave me the drive to do things I might not have otherwise, it also kept me needing something to rebel against and overcome so I could feel good about myself and continue to prove my worth.

On the positive side of the Princess, her gentle nature added softness, appreciation of beauty, an understanding of the need for compromise and a willingness to risk loving. Unfortunately, she was willing to risk a little too much for the cause, including her identity and sense of self.

Whether we look at archetypes from the mythological perspective, through Carl Jung's collective-unconscious approach or simply as a quick way to convey personality types, they are a great way to explore more about what makes us tick. Archetypes help show us how our greatest character attributes also hold the capacity to be our greatest flaws, so exploring them gives us a different way to discover the underlying limiting beliefs and programming that have kept us stuck in confusion and frustration.

So, who are you? Who are the archetypes calling the shots in your life?

I Was Almost a Beauty Queen

One way the conflict between the Princess and Rebel manifested in my life was at the end of my sophomore year in high school. At fifteen, my braces were gone, and so was some of my awkwardness, and I was considered pretty. When one of the guys from our football team was selected to play in the regional bowl game, he in turn had to choose a girl to go with him and compete for the title of Bowl Queen—and he picked me.

Princess was flying high, reveling in the pomp, pageantry and fairy-tale fantasy of it all, looking for the perfect dress and swimsuit and imagining herself as queen for a day. Then came the big weekend—the grand finale—it was time to get on stage and be royal.

Unfortunately, as with many big events, the process leading up to it was more fun than the actual doing. Turned out, while I was quite enamored with the *idea* of traipsing around in my layers of satin and lace, as well as a shapely swimsuit, actually *doing* it for the sole purpose of being looked at and judged was something else entirely. Also, not being in the know on the pageant world, watching the competition thing unfold was a bit disturbing. Seeing how seriously people took it—and how much drama and silliness they created because of it— made me ill. It also made me angry, which apparently was the cue for my Rebel to step up and take charge of the situation.

Wearing our swimsuits, high heels, satin banners and fake smiles, we beauty-queen wannabes posed as the judges eyed us up and down like heifers at the county fair, making notes on their clipboards about how we measured up—or not. Well, heifers at the fair was my first analogy, but it was not my last. Because, you see, the more Rebel thought about what Princess had gotten us into, the more peeved she became. Instead of gritting her teeth and smiling silently like a good little girl, she decided to share her thoughts. Within easy earshot of two of the judges, Rebel muttered—on purpose—that perhaps we should move things to the packing house down the road so we could have us a real meat show.

Yes, I said that. Yes, they heard it, and no, I did not win a sparkly crown for it—nor a 4-H ribbon. On the plus side, Rebel vowed never to let Princess get us into that sort of thing again. Never again would I slaughter my self-respect and dignity by pretending to be someone I wasn't. Never again would I turn myself inside out to try to convince others of my value...

Oops. Yes, it was a nice thought, but as you already know, it didn't play out that way. True, I never did any pageant things again, but what I did do was much worse. The behaviors that I'd felt disturbed, disgusted and demeaned by at the heifer show were the very ones that ruled my life. I went on stage every day, doing whatever was required to try to win validation from a man and prove myself worthy and lovable. Ouch.

Eventually, I came to realize that while both Rebel and Princess were aspects of me, I hadn't ever seen the whole picture of either—I'd only seen parts. Once I understood that all archetypes have positive and negative aspects—and beliefs that fuel them—I started seeing things differently. I realized that I could focus on the positive attributes of each and use them to my advantage. I could stop the internal squabbling and get them working together. The strengths of one could compensate for the weaknesses of the other. Taking the best traits of each, I could create a team that worked together to get us what we all wanted—joy.

Now, I love having the happy Rebel to call on to handle the seemingly impossible tasks, but struggle is no longer a defining factor in my life and I am not driven to constantly prove myself. I enjoy the girly ways of the Princess too, and I occasionally still indulge myself with one of her amusing romantic fantasies, but I neither need nor want to be rescued and I know my happiness is up to me.

The two voices in my head that were once mortal enemies have grown up to be best friends who support each other. When Rebel feels threatened and insecure and slips into the shadows, proclaiming she doesn't need anyone or anything, the Princess helps her remember that it's okay to let others help from time to time. And when the Princess feels overwhelmed and afraid, the Rebel reminds her of all the things she's done for herself and how strong and capable she really is. Just like any great relationship, together they are more than the sum of their individual assets, and that is way better than any fairy tale.

The Archetype Angle

We all have a host of archetypes that play roles in our personality. Some are prominent like my Rebel, and others are in the background, coming out only in certain situations. Self-discovery through archetypes can be a lot of fun as well as insightful, and there are many ways to approach it. Joseph Campbell's mythological approach is classic, as is Carl Jung's psychological one. I also really like *The Writer's Journey* by Christopher Vogler—even though it's for writers—because it uses familiar movies to explain how archetypes work in our lives and how we are each living our own Hero's Journey. They all go to the same place—self-understanding—they just use different ways and words to get there.

If you don't want to dive into a lengthy study, a quick way to start discovering what archetypes might be at work in your own life is by looking at character traits. Think about the traits and characteristics you most appreciate and value—as well as those you despise—then explore the different types that embody them. If you admire people who take risks, look at the Explorer, Adventurer and Gambler. If you appreciate the beauty of nature, you might look at Gardener, Artist, Photographer or Environmentalist, depending on your particular interest. On the other hand, if you can't stand people who are dishonest, explore the Liar, Thief and Charlatan.

Don't forget to look at both sides—the positive and negative—of each archetype. Honesty was on the top of my values list—I hated liars! Yet, when I explored a bit further, I realized that I was one of the biggest liars on the planet. I lied every day of my life. No, I wasn't deliberately dishonest to others, but I sure lied to myself. It was a coping strategy to help me pretend I was happy. So, look at all aspects, because the important insights can show up in places you wouldn't automatically expect—and where you'd prefer they didn't!

Another way is to look at occupations. We all know people who are teachers, but how many of them embody the Teacher archetype? Conversely, do you know someone who doesn't teach by trade but is an amazing example of Teacher? By looking at jobs, you start with form and function then expand into traits, characteristics, values and ideals.

There are a million and one archetypes, and they aren't limited to explorers, teachers, warriors, wizards, kings, queens, clowns and the like. Saying someone is a "Mr. Fix-It" tells us instantly that the person is handy, can fix just about anything and enjoys troubleshooting. The shadow side might be that he's always tinkering instead of completing projects. Whatever approach or labels you choose, be creative and find your own meanings that bring insights.

One of my favorite approaches to archetypes is from Caroline Myss's *Sacred Contracts*, which helped me realize the Princess and Rebel aspects at work in my life. I especially like Myss's perspective that we all have four primary archetypes we must make peace with: Child, Victim, Prostitute and Saboteur.

I certainly understood the victim aspect of my personality—why I'd developed it and how it had manifested in my life. It was also clear how I'd sabotaged myself. In both cases, I was replaying old patterns, and the traps I set for myself sabotaged any chance I had of breaking them and set me up to keep being victimized. On the positive side, once you get clear of the shadow aspects, Victim and Saboteur can serve as diligent sentries to keep you alert to situations of victimization and sabotage so you can avoid them.

The Child took me the longest to figure out. I could see where I had the positive aspect of having childlike wonder, which, as anyone who's had to endure my exuberance over some new experience will attest, I am full of. The shadow side, however, is being child*ish*. That, I believed, simply did not apply to me. When I had to own up to that one, it was highly unpleasant, to say the least. But owning it—and realizing why I was stuck there—gave me the insights and motivation to get out of it.

The Prostitute was the hardest for me to embrace. With my upbringing and programming, the last thing I wanted to do was be called a whore—that equaled death to my subconscious. Unfortunately, as I faced up to reality, I had to admit that's exactly what I was. I might have taken myself out of the sale barn at the beauty pageant, but I'd prostituted myself every single day in my marriage and the rebound relationship after it. I'd exchanged some part of myself—my identity, my dreams, my body and my self-respect—for the illusion of security and façade of self-worth. No matter what lofty spin I put on it my head, the women on the street corner were more honorable than I was. At least they were honest about what they were doing.

As you can see, it isn't always pleasant to discover things about yourself, but I promise once you get past the tough stuff, it can become fun. So, let's do a little exploring!

TRANSFORMATION INSIGHT **8**

Positive Traits

List the character traits that you value most by finishing this phrase:

I value someone who is _____

Trait or quality you value	Why
1.	
2.	
3.	
4.	
5.	

Examples: adventurous, artistic, athletic, attractive, calm, clean, clever, considerate, courageous, dependable, determined, dignified, educated, elegant, emotionally stable, environmentally conscious, ethical, extravagant, frugal, fun, funny, generous, glamorous, healthy, honest, intelligent, kind, a leader, loyal, mathematical, mature, mentally healthy, metaphysical, methodical, musical, neat, organized, passionate, physically strong, poor, pretty, quiet, religious, reserved, respectful, self-educated, simple, skilled, smart, spiritual, stable, successful, talented, thrifty, thoughtful, trusting, trustworthy, visionary, wealthy, well-dressed, well-groomed, witty.

Negative Traits

List the character traits that you find most offensive by finishing this phrase:

I am offended by or don't like someone who is _____

Trait or quality you find offensive	Why
1.	
2.	
3.	
4.	
5.	

Examples: an addict, adulterous, arrogant, a betrayer, boring, bossy, a bully, careless, cheap, a cheat, critical, dirty, dishonest, disorderly, disorganized, disrespectful, egotistical, extravagant, fanatical, flirtatious, greedy, a hoarder, ignorant, inconsiderate, insecure, irresponsible, judgmental, always late, lazy, a liar, narcissistic, narrow-minded, needy, oblivious, old, predatory, pretty, rude, selfish, self-centered, slow, a spendthrift, stubborn, stupid, ugly, uneducated, unethical, unkempt, unkind to animals, vain, vulgar, wasteful, young.

Archetypes

What mythical archetypes do you identify with? List five and explain why.

Archetype	Why you identify with it
1.	
2.	
3.	
4.	
5.	

Examples: Damsel in Distress, Knight, Fool, Martyr, Child, Storyteller, Warrior, Explorer, Fixer, Clown, Beggar, Gambler, Rescuer, Judge, Vampire, Advocate, Teacher, Healer, Wizard, Witch, King, Queen, Princess, Victim, Mother, Addict, Student, Slave, Nurse, Shaman, Writer, Performer, Trickster, Prostitute, Comedian, Magician.

There are positive and shadow aspects to each, so don't get attached to one because it seems noble and reject another because it seems bad. Be honest about what you really think and feel—it's just between you and you.

CHAPTER 9

WHERE'S THE REMOTE?

*Our behavior is just as predictable
and automatic as the television's.*

"Oh, she knows just how to push my buttons!"

How many times have you heard that? How many times have you *said* that? We all know what it means—or do we?

When someone "pushes your buttons" and you respond by giving that person a piece of your mind or perhaps an appropriate hand gesture, do you feel better? Do you feel vindicated? Have you shown her a thing or two? Does he know better than to do that to *you* again?

Well, you might feel better in the moment, or *for* a moment, but you probably don't feel peaceful inside. Odds are that your action didn't change anything either. Flipping someone off or otherwise getting revenge does not instantly align the stars so that no one ever pushes your buttons again. As long as you have buttons, somebody somewhere is going to push them. As long as you automatically respond to particular things in particular ways, you will keep getting those particular experiences.

Think of the way a television works. If you want to raise the volume, you push a specific button on the remote. If you want to change the channel, you push another. You know exactly what buttons to push to get the TV to do what you want, and it responds instantly and

75

consistently to your commands. And, as we all know, he who holds the remote controls the show.

We're all kind of like televisions with remote controls. We each automatically and unfailingly do what our particular remote tells us to, based on the button pushed. The TV doesn't have to think that someone is pushing the volume control, it just responds according to the programming of the electrical impulse from that particular source. Our programming works the same way. When we receive a programmed input, we react instantaneously in the way that's associated with that button every time. Our behavior is just as predictable and automatic as the television's.

Take a very basic example, such as a hug. Some people are huggers. They love giving and getting hugs. To them, it is a loving and caring thing to do and is as natural as breathing. Other people would rather be whacked with a stick than submit to a hug. They don't like it and no good can come of it. Try it, and they might freeze like a statue, push you away, or even flee. Whatever the reaction, it would happen before they consciously realized what they were doing or why. You might have thought you were pushing their "return loving feelings" button, because that's what your hug button is connected to. But the hug button on their remote control is wired to "fight, flight or freeze," and the results are not going to be what you were hoping for.

Each of us has different mental, emotional and physical reactions to situations. These reactions are automatic, and those people may not even realize that they have an aversion to being hugged, let alone why. Whatever the case, awareness of these kinds of triggers provides amazing opportunities for growth and improvement—on both sides of the fence. So, whenever you feel your buttons being pushed, just remember that it's your choice to go with the automatic reaction or to choose a different, conscious response. If you hand over your remote and allow that button to be pushed, you *will* act accordingly. You will feel the same old emotions and you will behave in perfectly predictable ways. You will also probably regret it later. I always do.

Road Ragers

You know how it goes. You're driving along, minding your own business, then some idiot whips out from nowhere and pulls in front of you. You're going sixty and he's barely moving. You slam on the brakes and somehow manage not to hit the fool. You curse and make a pointed hand gesture as emotion and adrenaline rush through you. He tootles on down the road, completely oblivious to—and totally unconcerned about—the near-death experience he just caused you. Your heart is racing; you're furious! Didn't the idiot realize he nearly killed you both? And, if you're really, really mad, you might even race in front of him and slam on *your* brakes just to show him how it feels.

I'd like to tell you that I have never done such a thing, but it would be a lie.

There was a time when I was really angry. I hated my life and I wanted out of it, but I wasn't strong enough to do what I knew I needed to do. I felt trapped and didn't believe that I could take care of my children and myself alone, so instead I stayed and seethed. I think what made me the angriest was that I'd set my own trap. I'd quit school, quit my job and had three kids. With no degree and no work experience in a decade, I had methodically stacked the deck against myself, ensuring that it would be virtually impossible to leave my marriage. So, I found ways to express my anger that had nothing to do with the actual source of my problem. Just about anything could trigger me, but the most reliable and frequent source was Colorado mountain driving.

I lived in the mountains west of Denver at the time and had a lot of kids and horses and such to cart around, so I drove a very large and heavy three-quarter-ton Suburban. I was barely visible behind the steering wheel when I drove it, but I loved the sure-footed behemoth and felt very safe on the icy mountain roads, invincible even.

But there were problems. I could be driving along, minding my own business, and out of nowhere, a car would appear on my bumper.

I'd look in my rearview mirror and all I could see was a slice of windshield and a roof. Being a vigilant, conscientious and thoughtful driver, I can't tell you how many times I was forced to slam on my brakes to alert the other driver that he was following at an unsafe distance.

Of course, tailgating wasn't the only issue I had to deal with on the roads. Merging into one lane of traffic in construction zones and during rush hour was a veritable wonderland of vein-popping opportunities. The place was littered with inconsiderate, self-absorbed people cutting in and zooming around on the shoulder to force their way in farther up the line. Some of us got wise to them and tried to keep them from going around by driving partly on the shoulder, but that didn't stop them. They just drove off the road and passed anyway. Much honking and saluting ensued from all sides, but I felt gloriously righteous at having dutifully carried my share of the burden of trying to make people do the right thing.

It isn't a pretty picture, is it?

Outside Mirrors, Inside Truths

So, what was really going on with me back then? If you'd asked me at the time, I would have told you that I hated where I lived because of the cold and the snow and the inconsiderate, selfish people who seemed to be everywhere. I would have told you that I'd never wanted to be there in the first place and that what I wanted hadn't ever mattered. I would have gone on and on with my story of victimization as long as you would listen.

With that in mind, it makes perfect sense that I would view the world on the road as I did. The big Suburban gave me a way to level the playing field. Behind the wheel, I might be invisible, but the vehicle wasn't—*it* couldn't be ignored. In the case of the people merging, it simply wasn't fair. They weren't letting me have my turn. *My* needs and desires didn't matter. What everyone else wanted came first, and I just kept getting pushed farther and farther back in the line—a scenario that perfectly mirrored what was going on at home.

On the road, however, I had some measure of control. If I slammed on the brakes or took up two lanes, I could *make* the wrongdoers do right. It might only be for a few seconds, but it made me feel that I had at least a little bit of power over something in my life.

From these examples, it is pretty easy to see that I was very unhappy and running on emotional overdrive. I couldn't face the truth about my situation, so I found ways to address it externally. They certainly weren't good ways, but they kept me focused on externals as the "problem," so I didn't have to deal with the real issue or make any changes in my life. I needed those experiences. I needed something to be mad at, and I was just begging for someone to push my buttons so I could have a "legitimate" excuse to vent the anger that I couldn't otherwise. It was my way of blowing off steam. It was also a way to tolerate what I knew I needed to change.

I don't know what deep inner needs were being served by those who were tailgating or cutting ahead in traffic any more than they knew why I was compelled to try to keep them from it. We were all just swapping emotional remote controls as we acted out our own personal subconscious dramas.

My intent in sharing these stories from my dark times is to help you see how my wounds manifested and created more pain in my life. I hope that seeing the connection between my inner and outer worlds will help you connect the dots between yours, right now, rather than years from now. I want to give you something that can help you shave some miles off your journey—something that can help you detour past the potholes that I stayed stuck in for a long time.

So, what pushes *your* buttons?

TRANSFORMATION INSIGHT 9

Think of a situation where you had an intense burst of emotion, such as anger, jealousy or even self-pity, and answer the following questions. You're looking for the reason beneath the reason, so dig deep.

1. Identify a situation where something triggered an intense response.

2. Describe what happened.

3. What were your first thoughts?

4. How did you feel?

5. What did you do?

6. How did you feel afterward?

7. Looking back on it now, how might the situation have been reflecting something you were struggling with internally?

8. Now that you realize that, how do you feel about your initial emotional response? Does it seem appropriate and necessary? Why or why not?

9. Knowing what you do now, how do you wish you had reacted?

10. How can you remind yourself of that option when you are in a similar situation?

CHAPTER 10

YOU BECOME WHO YOUR FRIENDS ARE

Those may be your limitations,
but they're not mine.

Yes, it's really true. You are—in some or many ways—just like the people you spend the most time with.

So, how do you feel about that? Do you believe it? What was your first thought when you read that allegation? Did you immediately think of a particular person? Did you smile? Did you recoil in horror? Get angry? Get worried?

If you didn't like how that statement sounded, stick around—it gets worse. Whether you realize it or not, you pick up mannerisms, speech patterns, beliefs and ways of viewing the world from those you consistently interact with—family, friends, co-workers, and so on. You may even do some of the same things others do that bug you the most.

Have you ever caught yourself speaking in a particular way because other people do? I don't even think about having a Texas accent—and I am really convinced that I don't until someone points it out—but when I go back there, I start using even more of my folksy phrases. I have friends in Colorado who swear my Texas accent is contagious and they catch it every time I'm around. Since I don't have an accent, I don't see how that's possible, but that's what they say—and they do kind of start talking funny . . .

Anyway, it can work with most anything. Have you ever been around someone with a distinctive habit, such as sucking their teeth, snapping their fingers, licking their lips or using a particular phrase, misusing or mispronouncing a word? You noticed it—may even have been annoyed by it—but just like my friends above, you later caught yourself doing it too.

We *all* do it. We adapt and become what we're around, and it influences what we do, how we think, how we communicate, what we talk about and how we talk about it.

So, take a step back and be your own observer. Think about how you interact with your friends. What do you talk about? How do you talk about it? Do you gossip? When you talk about others, what is the goal? As the observer, what view of the world would you say these people have? Do the friends encourage one another? Do they commiserate over a common enemy or problem?

As you go about your day, start paying attention to the conversations around you and the ones you participate in. You might be surprised at what is actually being said.

The following are some examples of typical conversations you may have heard before. You probably know some of these people: they're ones who not only see the glass as half empty, but expect that what's left in the glass is about to be tossed in their faces. They look for the negative in every situation, and they criticize everything and everyone. They can always find something worse to talk about than the last person. These people can suck the life right out of you. You can be whistling along, having a great day, and within seconds of talking to such a person, you feel horrible!

So, let's divide our Negative Nells into three groups: the One-Downers, the Happily Miserable and the Parade-Rainers.

One-Downers

This first example is of one-downing. It's similar to one-upping, except it's the art of coming up with something worse.

JUDY: *Hi, Brenda, how are you today?*

BRENDA: *Not so good. I think I'm coming down with something.*

JUDY: *Well, you're probably getting what I have. Every bone in my body aches. I've got sinuses going and my head is about to explode. It's probably the flu and I doubt I'll even be able to get out of bed by tomorrow.*

BRENDA: *You poor thing. Half the people over at the bank are out with it. That's probably what I'm getting, too, because I was just there. Of course, you know how this crazy weather is. It'll make you sick.*

JUDY: *It sure will. Why, it was freezing cold yesterday and now here it is hot as blazes. It's no wonder we're all feeling horrible. I just hope it's not one of those animal flu things they're always talking about.*

BRENDA: *Well, it wouldn't surprise me any. That's the way these things go, you know.*

This can—and will—go on . . . and on . . . and on . . .

I don't know how you felt reading that stuff, but it depressed me to have to write it. Nevertheless, we have to be fair to the guys and let them have a chat too.

JACK: *Hey, Ben, how's it going?*

BEN: *(heavy sigh) It's Monday, Jack. That's how it's going. It started out a Monday for me last night and it's going to be a Monday all day long. And if Bud doesn't get in gear and start making people do what they're supposed to, it's all going to fall on our shoulders, and it'll be Monday all week.*

JACK: *Boy, I know what you mean. After the weekend I had, I'm not going to put up with his crap today. I get so sick and tired of having to do his job for him. Is it some law that you have to be an idiot to be a boss?*

BEN: *Yeah, they send them to special MBA schools, although I'm the one who ought to have a "My Boss is an Ass" degree hanging on the wall.*

JACK: *(snickering) Not one of those pretty boys has a freakin' clue about what we do out here. This place would fall apart if it weren't for us.*

Have you heard conversations similar to this, and really, who hasn't? Have you participated in one? If we're honest, most of us would have to admit we have. However, I bet you won't do it again without remembering this unpleasant example.

If you consistently come away feeling bad after talking or being with a particular person, you've somehow fallen into a negative trap and the only way out is to stop talking for a while. No, it doesn't matter if it's your mother, brother or best friend. Just stop until you can get yourself in a better place and learn some techniques to keep you from diving back into the mud pits.

If you can take a break from talking to such a person for a week, do it. Notice how you feel during that week. Do you miss the interaction? What do you miss? What are you glad you don't have to deal with? Do you want to reconnect? Why or why not? Answering these questions will give you some amazing insights into the relationship dynamics you're participating in and the effects they've had on your life.

If you can't steer clear for a week, you're going to have to get tough—on yourself—and stop engaging in the negative conversation cycle anyway. If you've been a willing and active participant, your failure to fall into the expected negative pattern will not be received well, trust me. But if you want out, you're just going to have to figure out how to do it and not worry about whether someone gets mad about it.

Be gentle where you can, dodge and distract where possible and just keep changing the subject to something positive. There are tips and techniques in upcoming chapters that you can use to help things along, but changing patterns is not easy for anyone. Just remember, it's going to be very frustrating to the other person when you don't play the game as you always have. Not interacting in the normal—negative—ways will be uncomfortable for a while for both of you. They won't know what to do, and you won't either, until you get the hang of the new way of thinking.

Let's try the conversation with Ben and Jack again.

JACK: *Hey, Ben, how's it going?*

BEN: *It's Monday, Jack. That's how it's going (heavy sigh).*

JACK: *(jumps in during the sigh) Yeah, it sure is, and it's going to be a great one! A great Monday all day! (He waves, smiles and keeps walking.)*

I've actually done this on many occasions. It did not please the people on the receiving end, but it did please me!

The Happily Miserable

The receptionist at a company where I did quite a bit of work was the poster girl for the happily miserable. Why she was at the front desk and answering phones for that company, I never did understand. She shuffled around, groaning and mumbling, frustrated with her work, the people coming in to bother her and especially the ones calling in on the phone. How the phone stood up to the slamming was a mystery. Why the customers kept calling back was a bigger one.

I cringed every time I walked in the door, but nevertheless I always greeted her with a cheery hello. It did not get me a cheery hello in return—ever. Instead, she apparently considered it an invitation to share her personal dramas and woes. She did not, however, want help, only someone to unload on who would offer sympathy and a few "you poor thing" comments. At first, I didn't want to offend her, so I'd let her talk for a bit. When she took a breath, I'd offer her a positive spin on the situation or a different way of looking at it. She hated that and would immediately tell me why it wouldn't work out and how it never did, as well as a litany of other excuses people give when they really don't want solutions. I would then smile and say that I knew she would figure it out and do what she needed to do.

As time went on, I got better at stopping her more quickly and more gracefully. Eventually, I turned the tables on her completely by using preemptive strategies. I'd drop off a page of some uplifting and motivating materials or leave her a sticky note with a self-improvement website on it that I thought she might "enjoy." She did not, of course, and she eventually had nothing at all to say to me. She stayed miserable and I stayed free from a very dark cloud—and we were both happy.

Today, I wouldn't tolerate her behavior for two seconds, nor would I think I needed to help her. People who want help ask for it. And people who like being miserable don't want anyone trying to talk them out of it. So, steer clear and stay positive—no matter what.

Parade-Rainers

Do you know someone who can always come up with a reason why something won't work? These people come across as the absolute authority on everything and feel compelled to rebut or refute everything that didn't come from their own lips. To them, they're showing their brilliance and superior intellect. To others, they're showing something very different—fears, insecurities and perhaps their ass.

People who feel good about themselves aren't threatened by the ideas, success or even potential success of others, and they don't criticize. I'm not talking about genuine frustration or the occasional venting—we all need that—I'm talking about habitual patterns of fault-finding. People who are happy with themselves and their choices in life tend to be habitual about offering support and encouragement to those who are pursuing their dreams. The others carry around a chip on their shoulder and a bucket of cold water for everyone else.

If someone immediately starts shooting holes in your ideas, don't take it personally. Step back and consider why he might have said what he did. Constructive criticism can be very helpful, so you don't want to automatically bristle and miss a chance to improve. However, not all comments have good intentions behind them, so evaluate the situation carefully. Be grounded in reality, certainly, but don't let anyone dampen your enthusiasm for your own ideas. The fact that *they* can't do it or are afraid to try has absolutely nothing to with *you*!

If I'd waited for others to pronounce me competent, capable, educated enough or qualified enough, I'd never have done anything. I've heard "you can't do that" more times than I can remember. And most of those times, I did it anyway. One of my favorite responses is "Those may be your limitations, but they're not mine."

The reverse is true as well. My limited thinking may not apply to you, so I need to keep it to myself. The same goes for you. When someone else is expressing her ideas, dreams, goals or plans, let her. Even if you think it's the dumbest thing you've ever heard, is it really your job to say so? What do you know about it anyway? A lot of ideas that I consider dumb have made many people a lot of money. So, recognize that your opinion might simply be unnecessary limited thinking. Also, be kind. A thoughtful, objective observation can certainly be helpful—if asked for—but you can't go wrong by offering encouragement and support and sharing a person's enthusiasm for possibilities.

Think about it. We can rain on every parade—and maybe discourage people who could make incredible contributions to humankind—or we can encourage everyone to succeed in his or her dreams. Just as a rising tide raises all ships, each person's growth and joy enriches us all—it's how we build a better world. So, be the positive voice—you'll like it.

New Friends

We all want to be around people we resonate with, people whose ways of seeing the world and talking about the world are in alignment with our own. We want to be around people who make us feel comfortable and at ease. However, as we change, the people we click with will too—it's a good thing.

Ideally, a lot of your friends and family will come along and join you on the lighter and brighter side, but changing things up will take a little adjusting. In the meantime, you need your own network of support to keep you feeling good and moving forward. It's a whole lot easier to stay positive when you're around positive people, so start doing different things. Try something new, take an art or dance class, go to community events. A lot of people give free introductory presentations about their classes, programs or techniques, so go—you might like it. Attend a motivational seminar, personal development workshop or inspirational talk. Not only will you be inspired and motivated, but you'll also meet people who want the same things. Expand your way of looking at your world!

If we're meeting new people, and learning and doing new things, it means we aren't stuck. We aren't hopping on the same hamster wheel every day, running the same routines, scripts and ruts. We're having new conversations that involve more than talking about the weather or what someone else is doing. We're probably watching different television shows—if we even have time for such things. We aren't living vicariously through others—people we know or fictional characters, either one. We are *in* the world, not watching from the sidelines. We are actively creating our lives. We are *living*.

Who you share your world with is up to you. Hang around positive people who look for the good and you can't help but do the same, because you do become who your friends are. Choose wisely!

TRANSFORMATION INSIGHT

1. List the five people you spend the most time with.

2. For each person, list the topics that you generally discuss.

3. List the general feeling you have when you are "with" each person, face to face, by phone, by text or in cyberspace. Do you laugh? Get angry? Feel sad or hopeless? Feel energized and excited? Encouraged? Defensive?

4. List any speech patterns, phrases, mannerisms or gestures that you share.

5. Is this a predominantly positive or negative relationship? Why?

Name	Topics you discuss	How you feel with this person	Shared phrases or mannerisms	Positive or negative—why?
1.				
2.				
3.				

Name	Topics you discuss	How you feel with this person	Shared phrases or mannerisms	Positive or negative— why?
4.				
5.				

Now that you have a clear picture of how you interact with those closest to you, you can decide what, if anything, you want to do about it. You may see ways you can improve relationships by keeping conversations more positive, or you may realize you need to give yourself some space from perpetual negativity. Whatever the case, taking the time to realistically assess what kinds of friends you really have—and what kind of friend you are—can help you deal with situations more objectively and compassionately.

CHAPTER 11

THE FAMILY THAT PLAYS TOGETHER...

*Where is the rulebook that says you have to
show up so someone can abuse you?*

Friends are special, and to many of us, they *are* our family. But what if the most negative people in your life are the ones you've known since birth? What if the person who brings you down the most is your mother? Or your brother? What if it's your sister? Your spouse? And what if you're not quite ready to be disowned, divorced or dismembered just yet? Then what?

As the title of this chapter implies, the family that plays together keeps playing together—they act out the same old dramas they always have. Don't you know what to expect at a family gathering? Don't the same people generally do the same things? Bring up the same old stories? Start the same old squabbles? Susie has to run the show and tell people what to do. Jimmy has to pick at her about it, saying she's always been the favorite since she got piano lessons and he didn't. Mom defends the piano-lesson decision and reminds Jimmy he got the bicycle, which sends Susie into orbit—or whatever version of this nonsense works in your family.

Families have histories—no way around that. The same people have been saying the same kinds of hurtful things, right on cue, to one another for a very long time. Everyone has played their roles with their own agendas, hoping that somehow this time it will be different and they'll get what they never have before. So, how do we change it? How do *you* change it?

Well, it's pretty simple. Someone has to stop doing what she's always done, and that someone is you. As unpleasant as it is to admit, you've had your own starring role in the ongoing family drama just like everyone else. The issues might have originated in childhood, but they didn't end there. You have to own up to the fact that you've chosen—repeatedly—to be around people, and participate in situations, with a history of causing you pain.

Yes, It's Your Fault

I can hear you now: "Are you saying it's *my* fault that my mother criticizes me and makes me feel horrible?" In a word, yes. It *is* your fault that your mother *still* criticizes you and you *still* allow it and let it affect you.

If every time you're around your mother she says things that make you feel bad about yourself—and you choose to be around her and relate to her the way you always have—then yes, you *are* choosing to be criticized.

"Well," you say, "she's my mother and I have to—"

No, you don't. You could grow a spine and respectfully tell her she's not allowed to talk to you in that manner and that you're only going to talk with her about positive and uplifting topics. Or you could choose not to be around her. And, I have to ask, why do you want to anyway? Why do you want to be around someone who criticizes you, brings you down and otherwise causes you pain? Again, don't give me the "she's my mother" or "she's family." Where is the rulebook that says you have to show up so someone can abuse you?

Now, you can choose to be around a negative person—that's fine—just know why you're doing it and get your own boundaries clear in your head. You have to set the terms of what you'll tolerate and stick to them. If she doesn't like your new terms of endearment because she can't play her "here's why you're awful" tape, then she won't want to be around *you*. It's nothing personal, you just aren't giving her what she wants—an outlet to vent her unhappiness with herself.

But here's another option: get to the place where you no longer need her approval—you no longer need *anything* from her. Because really, the only reason any criticism from any source hurts is because there is a part of you that believes it's true. Once you are truly okay with yourself—once you've owned your warts and are doing your best to be your best—it no longer matters what someone else says.

Green Hair

I love Anthony Robbins's talk about green hair from his *Personal Power* series. To paraphrase his example: If I say you have green hair, it won't bother you because you know you don't have green hair. But if I say you're selfish and inconsiderate, and you hold that belief about yourself—even at an unacknowledged level—you'll feel bad, get angry or become defensive.

Think about it. What could someone say to you that would make you feel bad or mad, or make you want to explain, defend or return criticism? What if someone said, *"You're fat... you're skinny... you're ugly... you're mean... you're worthless... you're stupid... you never do anything right"*? If any of those phrases caused you to flinch—even a little—it's because there's some part of you that believes it's true.

So, if Mom's criticisms still hurt, it's because you've taken on her words as truth and have given her power over how you feel about yourself. Stop it. Get busy finding out why you feel that way about yourself and then start changing those beliefs. When you no longer need her approval, when you can smile at her criticisms, hug her and tell her you love her anyway no matter what she thinks, that's when you'll know you're over it. Because then you'll have realized that her criticisms have nothing at all to do with you and neither does her withholding of anything. Her behaviors are about *her* fears and limiting beliefs—her wounds and baggage.

Once you've made that shift in your head—once you have your power back—you can never look at her in the same way ever again, because you no longer need anything from her. You don't need her approval, because you have your own. There's nothing she can withhold that you need to survive, because you already have everything within. When you have reclaimed your power, she has none over you, and whatever she says or does is just drama she's creating for herself—not for you.

And, who knows, once you've changed the rules of the game, it might even inspire her to make some positive changes as well. You can't count on it, however, and you certainly have no control over it. What she does is up to her, and what you do is up to you. So, take care of you and do what you need to in order to be the best and happiest *you*.

Mommy Dearest

I saw a reality show where a group of young women were facing issues with their parents and were required to write a letter to each as part of their emotional process. On the episode I watched, each girl had to write a letter to her mother, telling her how she'd affected the daughter's love life.

I've done similar exercises myself with the same goal of getting to the bottom line of reality—mine and my mother's—and making peace with it. Listening to the girls read the letters they had written brought home both sides of the equation for me: the daughter who'd been damaged and the mother who had passed on her own pain. I was both—just as my mom had been.

It made me wish my daughters would write their own unpleasant letters to me, because I don't want them going through their lives with "mother" baggage hanging over their heads as long as I did. As horrible as this is to admit, there was a time—a very long time—when I believed I couldn't really live my life until my mother was no longer living hers. It's an awful thing to have to confess, but it's also very true.

Well, let's clarify exactly what part is "true." It was true that I felt and believed it. However, it wasn't even remotely true that her death was going to magically make the problems I blamed her for go away. And believe me, it didn't. Neither will writing a letter. But what writing a letter *will* do is help you face your own truths—the ones you know about and the ones you've been pretending you don't—the problems that your mother can't fix no matter what she does.

The great thing is, while getting your truth out in the open may not be pleasant—and it may even be really ugly, as mine was—there's a huge relief once it's done. It's kind of like ripping off that bandage and cleaning the wound—it hurts while you're doing it, but once you've done it, it no longer has power over you, you can see it for what it is and you can start to heal.

Now, be aware that writing a letter or otherwise confronting a parent is not a magic bullet that will instantly fix anything—it won't. In fact, just because you write the letter doesn't mean you need to share it. If your mom is still in denial about her own pain, she might automatically react to defend herself, explaining why you shouldn't feel what you feel, and crush your newfound courage in the process. At least that's what happened to me every time I tried confronting my mother—and when I replayed that same disempowering pattern on my own children.

So, think about what you want to do with the letter. Some people burn them. Others keep them until they no longer need them. Some do share them. Whatever you do, just be clear on why you're doing it. If you burn it, do it on purpose and with intent, such as freeing yourself from the past. If you keep it, be sure you know why you want to. Is it so that you'll never forget what she or he did to you? Or so you can remember how you resolved your pain?

If you think you want to share it with the person who hurt you, be really clear on why. Do you want your mom to know how what she did was wrong and how it made you feel? Do you want understanding? An apology? Do you think reading it and knowing how you feel will change her and she'll finally love you the way you want her to? Get clear on the outcome you want—what you want her to do and why, and whether it's a realistic expectation.

Remember, you didn't come up with your wounds by accident, and your mom could still be protecting herself from a version of the same pain you have. You can't expect to get understanding and validation of your pain from the very person you blame for creating it. Unless she's done her own work, odds are that your mom's own fragile self-concept will demand that she convince you that you're wrong to feel as you do. So, be very careful if you choose to go there. You don't have to.

The letter writing is for you—to clear your slate and make peace. Your parents may have helped create your baggage, but you are the only one who decides whether you keep dragging it around with you. As we talked about earlier in the chapter, you don't need anyone's approval, validation, cooperation or even awareness in order to heal. You've got everything you need to take care of that yourself.

You can't get from another person what you can only give yourself, so look at your letter carefully and see what you're really needing. Read between the lines and find the deeper meaning of your requests. If you want an apology, why? Do you think if your mom says she's sorry she wasn't there for you or didn't love you in the ways you needed, you'll know that it wasn't your fault—that you really were lovable and worthy of being cherished? Do you think if she admits she didn't protect you, you'll forgive yourself for not being able to? Will you finally believe that you've always been worth protecting? Will you finally feel worthy and lovable just because you're you? Feel it anyway.

When you break free of needing something from your mom to feel okay about yourself, you change the whole dynamics of the relationship. Since you no longer want something from her, there's nothing for her to resist. She can still feel defensive and in pain—that's her deal and her choice—but you won't be feeding into it. It won't tie you up in emotional knots. It won't control your life anymore.

And the really great thing is that when you heal, you won't pass along those old patterns and pain to your children. So, make a vow right now to stop that family tradition and start a new one—giving yourself what you've spent your whole life waiting to get from others. Pass *that* on!

TRANSFORMATION INSIGHT 11

Here are a few questions to help you gain some insights into your family dynamics. Ignore the fact that you know you need to give these things to yourself and explore how you might get it from others. It sounds counterintuitive, but it isn't. Once you are honest about what you need from others—or thought you did—you will have a much better idea of what to do for yourself. Get as petty as possible. There is nothing too small to address. If you feel it, acknowledge it.

1. What is the one thing you feel like you never get (e.g., validation, support, unconditional love, acknowledgement of your ideas/skills/creativity, feeling special)?

2. How do you feel because you don't get that?

3. How do you think you would feel if you did?

4. What would someone have to say or do to make you feel that way?

5. Who would you most like to do that?

6. What is one thing you've always wanted your mother, father, spouse, child or another person to say to you that they never have? Describe how you'd feel if they did.

7. What words of approval do you long to hear?

8. What would it mean if that person said exactly what you've always wanted to hear? What would change?

9. What wrongs do you want a particular person to admit to?

10. How would it change things if they admitted how they wronged you?

11. If you were able to tell your mother, father, spouse, child or other person your whole and complete truth about a troubling situation with them, what would you say?

12. Describe the way you most frequently wind up in an unpleasant situation with a family member. How you can disengage from the drama and interact differently?

13. Use your answers to the questions above to make a list of all the things you need to give yourself.

14. List the beliefs about yourself you need to change in order to do that.

15. What are some techniques you've already learned that can help you get solid in your own self-worth and stay disconnected from the opinions of others (e.g., two-question litmus test, green hair, carrots and sticks)? Be specific and play out sample scenarios. Take the time to do it. You're worth it!

BONUS INSIGHT: Write a letter to your each of your parents and/or other significant family members, telling them what you appreciate about them and what you wish they'd done differently. Explain how their actions have affected your life and how what they did—or didn't do—made things difficult for you and caused you pain.

CHAPTER 12

JUDGE, JURY AND JOLLY JOKERS

---

*We can never know what's going on
in others' heads; all we can ever know for sure
is what the situation triggers in us.*

I knew a woman who seemed to laugh and carry on all the time, to act solicitously toward everyone, and to be considerate and caring. In some ways, those things were true—she did do nice things for people—but it didn't take long to figure out that it was only because she wanted them obligated to her. She expected that because she had done something for a person, he or she owed her, and she would say so, but always in a joking way.

When I really started paying attention, I realized that most of her comments were either delivering a judgment or soliciting one. And even though she always seemed to be laughing and making jokes, she was also criticizing and making demands. She meant what she said—it wasn't teasing or pretend—she just said it as a joke to get her point across so no one would get mad about it, at least not openly.

After I got to know her better, I began to understand that she was really a very unhappy, insecure woman who didn't like herself and was constantly measuring herself against everyone else. When she commented that someone was too fat to be wearing a particular kind of shirt, she was really thinking of her own body and weight. When she criticized someone's hair, she was reflecting deep criticisms and worries about her own. She didn't feel good about herself, so how could she see anything good in anyone else?

The Way I See It...

When you judge another's behavior, it is always with your own measuring stick—based on your particular experiences and beliefs. That's why there's so much misinterpretation of things. We all see things a little bit differently—even the same things.

Do you know someone who is color-blind? They may see purple as brown, and green may look brown too. No matter what you say, no matter how hard you try to convince them, they just won't be able to see things your way. Granted, that's a physical issue, but the point is that we all have our filters. We've had different experiences, and even different outcomes from the same experience, so when we see a situation, it's always through our own customized lens.

An eye-opening example of this came when a friend and I were checking out at a shop downtown. A man and a woman stood nearby, looking at a jewelry display. He was insistent on buying her something and she was equally insistent that he wasn't going to.

Within a few seconds of being near the couple, I knew something was not right. The situation felt horribly uncomfortable for me, and I wanted to run far and fast and take the woman with me. My friend, on the other hand, was just annoyed. She muttered, "Oh, for crying out loud, just say thank you."

I don't know what ultimately happened—or why—and there are a thousand possible scenarios. It really doesn't matter what *their* story was, because it was never about them. No, the judgments my friend and I put on the couple were about us—our own beliefs, assumptions and issues.

Luckily, we had enough understanding of that to be able to look at the situation, as well as our automatic reactions to it, and use it to learn something about ourselves. I asked her why she'd said what she did, and, basically, her take on it was that the woman wasn't willing to accept a gift—she wouldn't allow others to give to her. My perception, on the other hand, was that the man was trying to buy the jewelry to obligate the woman to him and put her in a position she didn't want to be in, and it looked to me like she was on the verge of panic about it.

We'll never know what was going on in either of their heads. All we can ever know for sure is what the situation triggers in us. My friend's view of it makes total sense when you understand that she is a giver—she is always doing something for someone—and she is not so good at letting someone do for her.

For me, the situation set off all kinds of alarm bells that a woman was about to have to do something she didn't want to do. She had to either accept the gift and the obligation that went with it or forcefully decline, hurt the man's feelings and risk him not liking her. From where I stood, no good was coming from it for her, for the rest of the evening or maybe for the rest of her life.

Sounds melodramatic, or perhaps even silly, but that's what went through my head and what I felt. And believe me, I felt it as if it were me standing there with the guy instead of her.

These kinds of experiences aren't silly, but they can make us feel ashamed of having them, which makes us tend to ignore our thoughts and feelings. And, as we know very well by now, understanding those thoughts and feelings is the key to the happiness castle. My friend's "just say thank you" advice and my "run and run fast" judgment were important messages to share—with ourselves. When we project them on others, however, we miss vital opportunities to clear out our own garbage that's keeping us stuck.

There's a big difference between judging the situation and using it as an opportunity for self-awareness. *"Did you see what she did… That's the dumbest thing I've ever heard… She ought to…"* and the like are very different thought processes from *"Did you just see what happened? Here's the perception and reaction it triggered in me. Wonder why that is?"* Big huge difference. One pays big dividends of personal insight. The other is just gossip.

All About You or Me?

A reader sent me a great question the other day, wondering why the same kind of people kept showing up in her life. "If you're overrun with 'all about me' people," she wondered, does that mean you're one too? The short answer is—maybe or maybe not.

The way I look at it, there are several possible reasons why the same type of person keeps showing up. Here are some options to consider:

1. Mirror: The undesired characteristic is an unacknowledged part of yourself that you need to face, and seeing it in others is the first step to seeing it in yourself. It may not be a perfect reflection, but if it really bugs you, there's something that you need to take a closer look at and own up to.

2. Haven't Let It Go Yet: The behavior or characteristic is one you're aware of and have worked to eliminate, but you haven't fully let go of it because it represents a familiarity (or a family tie) that is difficult to give up. For example, I kept finding myself in sticky situations with negative people that there seemed no good way out of. For one reason or another, I felt forced to maintain some kind of relationship or risk serious consequences, such as losing my job or being ostracized. In my case, it was a replay of the situation with my mother and her negativity, along with the unresolved issues of loss and guilt.

3. Wish I Could: The characteristic or quality is one you secretly wish you had—or one you need. Even if it's manifesting as a negative thing to get your attention, the message can be that you need to embrace the positive side of the quality you're resisting. If you feel you're surrounded by "all about me" people, maybe *you* need to be more self-honoring. Maybe it's time for you to be a little "all about you" for yourself in a positive way. While the way these people are acting may feel offensive to you, it could be that they are showing you how you aren't taking care of your own needs.

4. Something's Wrong Somewhere: The situation is a warning sign that things are not all right in your world no matter how much you will argue that they are. Back in my own dark days, I vehemently swore to anyone who'd listen that I was happy, happy, happy—and I'd bite the head off anyone who dared suggest otherwise. During that time, I was constantly being treated badly by everyone. Store clerks ignored me, overcharged me or made me feel insignificant. I couldn't pull out of my driveway without someone tailgating, cutting me off, pulling out in front of me going 10 miles an hour or otherwise putting their needs before mine and not giving a hoot. I wasn't doing those same things, but they were real-world reflections of how I felt in my own life at home.

5. Bad Apples: These are just selfish people being themselves and you don't have to feel bad about not wanting to be around them. And maybe that's the whole point of the experience—to push you so you'll do something about it. So, grow a pair and stop putting up with things you don't have to.

These options should give you some things to think about and help you home in on the bottom line for your situation. You'll know it when you find it—it will feel right. Once you do, then you have to figure out what you want to do about it. As we've already discussed, if you've struggled to clear out your own negative ways, it's really hard to stay positive around people who bring you down. But once you know why they bring you down, the "what to do" part is easy. Once you disengage, the dynamics of your interactions must change. They'll either start respecting your feelings—because you have—or they'll find someone else who'll tolerate their narcissistic behavior.

So, yes, it really *is* all about you—as it should be!

Stop the Madness

The bottom line is, if you want others to treat you differently, start treating yourself differently. If you don't like being around selfish, judgmental and negative people—don't.

People who are chronic complainers and criticizers are not happy people, and they keep their focus on judging others so they don't have to face their own demons. Focusing on the faults of others allows them to feel smug and superior, their own warts safely hidden—or so they think. And here's another bottom line: The only people who will tolerate chronic criticizers and complainers are criticizers and complainers.

So, if you're always busy finding fault with others, stop it. Shift your focus away from what others are doing and onto what you're doing. The easiest way to stay stuck and unhappy is to be looking at how others need to fix themselves and their lives. Start being the person you think everyone else ought to be. Walk your own talk. Take responsibility for the way things are in your life. Putting up with unacceptable behavior doesn't make you "good," it makes you a doormat. When you respect yourself, others will too. If you want different outcomes, make different choices.

In the next chapter, you'll get some specific tips on dealing with negative people and others who drive you crazy. First, however, let's get some more insight on who those people are and what kinds of problems they cause.

TRANSFORMATION INSIGHT 12

List three things (e.g., situations, people, feelings) that you recall complaining about most recently and what bothered you most.

Situation/Person/Feeling	What bothered you most
1.	
2.	
3.	

List the types of people you tend to attract in your life that you wish you didn't. Describe how they annoy you, how they cause you problems and how it all makes you feel—about them and about yourself.

Type of Person	Why they annoy you, how they cause you problems, or how it makes you feel
1.	
2.	
3.	
4.	
5.	

You can use the character traits list you made in Chapter 8 to give you some ideas, if needed.

13 SANITY-SAVING STRATEGIES

Get clear on your motivations and it will be much easier to make wise decisions that are truly helpful to others—and that are respectful to yourself.

Now that you have a list of people and situations that drive you crazy, you'd probably like to know what to do about them. Since there are laws against all the fun stuff that comes to mind—and simply putting up with their nonsense is just as unacceptable—you need something to help keep you sane.

This chapter has thirteen tips and techniques just for that. You'll get specific ways of dealing with negative people, annoying people and the happily miserable Gray Cloud Crowd.

When you learn different ways of dealing with the Negative Nells of the world, you'll feel better. They won't push your buttons and you won't take their antics personally, because they aren't. They're just being who they are and doing what they do. As this next story shows quite clearly, it's their nature.

1. Don't Play with Snakes

Many of you have probably heard Aesop's fable, "The Farmer and the

Viper." The story is told many ways, but here's the gist: A man sees a snake freezing in the snow and takes pity on him. He puts the snake under his coat to warm him up, and the snake revives and bites him. The man is shocked that his kindness has been repaid by an attack that could kill him. The snake, however, simply shrugs and says, "You knew I was a snake when you picked me up."

Dealing with human snakes works the same way.

I found myself in a situation with a woman a couple of years ago that I did not know how to handle. I figured out her nature pretty quickly—I knew she was a snake—but she was also an influential snake with the power to negatively affect a project I was working on, which she eventually, and cheerfully, did.

I let myself get lured in because I feared the consequences of not being friendly with her. I did things to be helpful and nice, but always—and I do mean always—it came back to bite me in one way or another. I kept playing the game with her, thinking that this time things would be different, this time she wouldn't act like a snake, this time she would appreciate how nice I was and would be grateful and kind in return. *This* time she would do the right thing. Well, she did the right thing, all right—from her point of view—and it had dramatic consequences for me.

I bet you've known a human snake or two in your life and have probably been surprised when your good intentions didn't get the results you expected. But if you think about it, who was really at fault? Was it the snake for being a snake? Or was it you for not being clear about your motivations for playing with the snake? Were you expecting your "goodness" to transform the snake into a grateful puppy who would then give you the appreciation and warm fuzzies you were looking for?

If you choose to befriend snakes, know why you're doing it. If it's really for the good of the snake—and if the snaking is asking for your benevolence—you can be helpful without putting yourself at risk. But if your goal is really to get gratitude and praise from the poor soul you've rescued—or if it's tied to your own personal fears in some way—there's probably a pretty hefty bite in your future, just as there was for me. Do not expect otherwise.

2. The 3-Ds—Dodge, Distract and Detour

Whether it's a holiday dinner, a wedding, a funeral, a party at work, a conference or a chance meeting in the grocery store, you can often find yourself having to deal with people you don't want to. Keeping your sanity intact and your private business private might be your goal, but pushy, nosy or negative people have other plans. So, what do you do?

Let's say you're at a family gathering and Aunt Edna has you in her sights. She's making a beeline in your direction and all possible exits are blocked—there is no escape. While you're considering just how bad it would be to body-slam Cousin Chris, leap over the twins in the stroller and flee the state, Aunt Edna appears in your face, smiling sweetly, saying, "Tell me, dear, is your husband still with that little tramp he left you for?"

Well, let's press the pause button on that happy scene and get one thing crystal clear. Just because someone asks you a question does not mean you have to answer it. When someone asks a backhanded question like the one above, it doesn't matter how sickly sweet the voice is, the intent is anything but. In this case, Aunt Edna is just being her nosy, judgmental self, and her concern has nothing to do with how you're holding up after your divorce. It's about being the first to get the juicy details—being the one in the know. She's also letting you know how superior she feels because she's stayed married to Uncle Ed for over forty years, making her better than you.

Now, you could inquire—just as sweetly, of course—about Uncle Ed's weekly overnight "fishing" trips or ask when was the last time the happy couple actually had a real conversation. You could call her out of her glass house if you wanted to—it might shut her up—but, as with the snake people above, it might just unleash more venom. If you'd like another option, here's the 3-D method. It might not be nearly as satisfying in the moment, but it won't leave you feeling slimy afterward. Instead of addressing Aunt Edna's probing question directly, slip on your 3-D glasses and Dodge, Distract and Detour your way out of it.

> **AUNT EDNA:** *Tell me, dear, is your husband still with that little tramp he left you for?*

> **YOU:** *(Start with a dodge) Oh, aren't you sweet. You were always thinking about me when I was growing up too. (Shift gears and distract) I remember every time I was at your house, you had brownies for me. It always made me feel special. I always loved those brownies, and I've wanted to ask you for the recipe for years. (Detour to something else) Would you share that with me?*

Now, Aunt Edna may recognize that you have avoided her question, but she can't gracefully go back to the dark side with you gushing over how wonderful she is. You dodged her question, distracted her with another topic and detoured everything to the positive side—and a new topic.

It took me a long time to realize that I didn't have to spill my guts just because someone was curious—and longer still to stop defending against the unspoken judgments that came with the nosy questions. When I got over worrying about being thought of as nice—or being shunned for not being so—it became a whole lot easier to see the situation for what it was. I realized I could have boundaries—I *needed* healthy boundaries—and I didn't have to put up with anything from anyone I didn't want to. I also realized I didn't have to be angry or fearful about it. That comes naturally when you start honoring and respecting yourself.

3. Make a Happy List

Since you may not always have a brownie-recipe memory on the tip of your tongue, do your homework and make what I call a Happy List. Write down the names of people you might run into at an event or during the holidays, then jot down an interest or a story that can serve as a get-out-of-jail-free topic-turner for each. At the bottom of the list, note a few general possibilities for positive conversation—no politics, religion, or sex—that you can use with just about anyone. Make the list and keep it handy. Do it—you'll be glad you did.

This is also a great technique for dealing with people over the phone. Whether it is an elderly parent or friend, or simply someone with whom you're trying to change a negative conversation pattern, make the list. Write down general topics of conversation that you think they might like to talk about—and that you can talk about well enough to keep things going. Make notes about something positive you saw on television or in the paper. Keep it with your phone, and when things stray into unpleasant territory, use it.

Avoid saying, "How are you?" or any version of that—ever. Avoid asking health-related questions of people who are perpetually focused on something being wrong their health. I'm not talking about some-one with a serious issue who needs support and encouragement in dealing with it. No, I'm talking about that person who always has aches and pains and never ever feels good—the one who's always run-ning to the doctor for something and always has a new pill. Do not, even casually, ask these people how they're doing—ever. No good can come of it. Trust me.

4. Ask a Question

This is an extension of the Happy List. As you've seen, you can use the 3-D technique to turn things around at any point. It works even if there isn't a question hanging in the air. If you find yourself trapped on the receiving end of a long, sad soliloquy, you can break in and ask a totally unrelated question to steer the conversation out of the muck and in a different, positive direction. That's where the Happy List comes in handy. As you think of things to ask about, add them to the Happy List.

As in the brownie example, you could break off a historical tale of woe by saying, "Hey, speaking of the old days, you just reminded me of something I've been meaning to ask you." Yes, you're interrupting, but you're implying that it is a good and important thing, urgent even, and it was her thoughtful commentary that triggered it. Once you've made the break, immediately jump in with your "Did you ever find that brownie recipe? You always have the best recipes, and I have so much fun trying them out." Using words like "you have the best" and "have so much fun" move the conversation into a completely different arena, and the person can hardly be mad when you're expressing good things about her.

5. Tell Me Something Good

Another way to shift a conversation with a habitually negative person is to say something like "I don't know about you, but I'm ready to talk about something good! Tell me something good that happened today." This can be tough for people who are used to focusing on the bad. They can itemize, characterize and emphasize every single thing that went wrong at the snap of their fingers, but go completely blank on the good stuff. So, be prepared to jump in if they can't think of anything to say. And if you can't think of anything either, grab your Happy List and improvise.

6. Get Over It

As we talked about in the last chapter, the best way to avoid replaying old dramas and subjecting yourself to the same unpleasantries is by getting over it. You don't have to get sucked back into the muck and find yourself saying and doing the same things you did the year before with the same dismal outcomes. You just have to do your mental laundry before you get there. We all want approval, validation and a sense of belonging from parents and family, but the fact is not all of us get it—and never will, no matter what we do. So, if you're still waiting for negative relatives to validate you, you're in for a long wait. Don't set yourself up to be miserable. Get over it and go prepared.

Do not for a second think that getting a third PhD is going to get you the "atta girl" you want from people who are disappointed you didn't join the family dog-grooming business. If they didn't jump for joy over the last two doctorates, this third one isn't going to do the trick either. It's not that they don't realize you've done something, they do. And what they realize is that you turned your back on their world and did something you think is better—better than what they do and better than they are. They don't understand what you're doing or why you did it, they just know they don't like the way they feel when you tell about it. You're just a big shot trying to make them feel bad, so they're going to do whatever it takes to feel good. Make sense?

I hope so, because it leads to the next technique, which is . . .

7. Do Not Talk about Yourself

The only reason negative people care about what you're up to is because they want something to ridicule, brag about or gossip about to make themselves look or feel good. Don't go there. Whether you just filed for bankruptcy or won a Nobel Prize, keep it to yourself. No good can come of it—none. You probably won't get the kudos you're expecting, but even if you do, what you're also going to get is your news—reconfigured in whatever way works for the teller—spread all over town, the office or the family. And why do you need to chatter like a chipmunk about yourself anyway? Might want to think on that one too.

We all like to share what we've been up to, but be very selective about what you say, who you say it to and how. We've probably all been in conversations where we weren't really listening, but just waiting for our turn to jump in and share our own thoughts. What good did it do? Was the person you weren't listening to immediately enthralled with what you had to say? I doubt it. Cutting off a long-winded blowhard is one thing, but just waiting until someone takes a breath so you can tell an even better story or explain how you know more isn't a good move. And, well, it kind of makes *you* the blowhard.

Everyone has a story, and even people you've known your whole life have tales to tell that you've never heard. Those from earlier generations have very different life experiences that you'll never know about unless you ask. Put aside your need to be important and start showing genuine interest in others. Draw them out and ask questions. Get them talking about things they've done or lived through or activities they're passionate about. Become genuinely interested in others, and you might be surprised what you can learn—and how much people enjoy you in return.

8. Do Not Share Your Woes

If you're not going to talk about yourself, it would seem obvious that sharing your woes would be off the table. However, when we're in a tough place, it can be easy to fall off the wagon and look for a shoulder to cry on. Well, that's what best friends and therapists are for.

Even in a weak moment, even when you've had the worst day ever—maybe especially then—talking about it with others at a group event is a bad idea. Saying *anything* about it to a negative person is a horrible one. You might get a microsecond of sympathy, but that's only so they can launch into telling you how much worse they have it or chastise you for your actions or feelings. And if you're going to share with one person in a group, you may as well grab a microphone and share with all of them. At least that way, you'll know they heard the correct details. So, unless you want to be the talk of the party, the family or the town, or hear advice or judgments you don't need, do not talk about your troubles.

9. Do Not Say Anything Negative—Ever

Again, this should be obvious, but it warrants a reminder. If you hear yourself criticizing, judging or complaining, you're part of the problem. If you're working on breaking out of negative cycles, you can step into a complainer snare and find yourself hanging upside down in the jungle before you realize it. So, stay aware and vigilant, and remember you can always take back control simply by thinking about what you choose to say—or not say.

10. No One-Downing

Remember this from Chapter 10? It's the opposite of one-upping. It's the art of coming up with something worse when someone else makes a negative comment or talks about a problem. No matter what negative thing anyone says, or how much you agree with it or don't, resist the urge to respond with another negative comment. When we're in a conversation, it is natural to match the flow with a similar statement. Our brains will go searching for something relevant. However, in these cases, the only thing relevant is something negative, so go for irrelevant and turn things around with your 3-D techniques.

11. End the Conversation

When you find yourself in a conversation that is making you feel irritated, aggravated, frustrated and possibly homicidal, the best thing to do is just cut things short. Use whatever means necessary, preferably while you still have the ability to appear somewhat sane.

On the phone, one way is the totally dishonest "I'm getting another call and I have to take it" or "Someone's at the door." Not a good way to handle things, but desperate times can require desperate measures, and it's better than blowing your cork.

I did that once, the cork blowing. To my mother. Yes, it was bad. She had been regaling me with her latest ailments and such and I just couldn't take any more of it. I believe she had a head cold, and about the third time she told me that "nobody knew" how she felt, I blew. I informed her that everyone on the planet knew how she felt. I don't know if I said anything more, because all I remember is stunned silence. Clearly, it was not one of my finer moments.

In my defense, that was a long time ago, and I didn't know what I know now. At that time, all I knew was that I wanted to be free of her dramas and negativity—the same dramas and negativity I'd heard from her my whole life. Now, of course, I wish I had a do-over, because I could handle things more compassionately without taking it personally. Then, all I had to work with was my own frustration and negativity.

The best I could have done was to just say nothing. I could have chosen to end the conversation. I wish I had.

12. Just Do Your Best

As Don Miguel Ruiz writes in *The Four Agreements*, in addition to being impeccable with your word, never assuming and not taking things personally, the final "agreement" we can make with ourselves is to always do our best. He also reminds us that our best varies with the circumstances. What's your best today might be far out of reach tomorrow.

So, as you go through this wonderful transformation process, just do your best. Hold yourself accountable, but don't hold too tightly. It's about being aware and being responsible, but you have to cut yourself some slack too. You also have to allow others the same latitude. We all make mistakes, and sometimes it can seem like a "two steps forward, one step back" process. I promise you, however, that it only feels that way for a short time. Sure, you'll continue to make mistakes, but you'll understand why and make adjustments accordingly much quicker. Your best will get better.

13. Share Your Gratitude

Another way to shift a negative into a positive is by being grateful. You've probably heard it before, but being grateful for what you have in your life opens the door for having more good stuff show up. Some people run down their list of things they're grateful for before they get out of bed in the morning and before they go to sleep at night. It's a good practice, helpful on many different levels and in many ways, including staying positive.

Appreciation is another word for gratitude. While we may find it easy to be grateful for the good stuff we have in our lives, we might not always be grateful for the people. We can, however, learn to appreciate them—or at least some aspects.

When we can find something good about another person and reflect those positive qualities back to him, it can shift the energy, tone and even direction of a conversation. Handled well, appreciation can turn an awkward or defensive situation into one of mutual respect and cooperation. It can also help an insecure, defensive person relax and peek out from behind her mask a bit. But what if you can't find a single thing to appreciate about someone?

A friend of mine who is a horse trainer and author tells a story about a stallion she worked with that she just had no use for. She didn't like him from the minute she saw him and things went downhill from there. Besides being her least favorite breed, he had a bad attitude, pig eyes, short ears, crooked legs and a litany of other problems that stood out to her like flashing neon signs. Needless to say, they did not have a good rapport and training was not going well.

Desperate to remedy the situation, she was aware enough to realize that there was no legitimate reason for her to feel as she did—so she made herself find something she *did* like about him. It took a while, but she finally noticed his tail. The more she looked, the more she realized that the horse had the most beautiful, long, thick tail she'd ever seen. *That* she could appreciate. Once she started see the horse through his tail, her attitude changed and so did their relationship. Once she found something to appreciate about him, he found something to appreciate about her.

It works the same way with people. If there are people you can't stand, look for something good about them that you can appreciate. Not their tails, probably, but maybe you appreciate how neat and orderly they are, or how they can remain calm under pressure, that they are always on time, how much they love animals, their ability to fix things, that they love their kids, mother, golf, opera—anything. And, if it's appropriate, share your appreciation. You might be surprised how things can shift—even if it's just for you.

TRANSFORMATION INSIGHT 13

Take a deep breath and let it all out, because this is an easy one. No deep digging this time, just some life-saving list making. Fill out both lists below and keep them with you. You'll be very glad you did. And when they do save your life—or at least your sanity—you'll be glad I kept pushing you to do it. Now, do it!

The first list is for strategies. Write down the techniques you think you'll use, where, when and with whom you'll use them, and how. Make any notes you need to so you'll remember these tips and be able to use them on the fly.

Sanity-Saver Strategies

Technique	When, where, with whom, and how
1.	
2.	
3.	
4.	
5.	
6.	
7.	

Make a Happy List. You can use this form here, copy it or make your own. Doesn't matter how you do it, just that you do it.

Happy List

Name or situation	Topic or question
1.	
2.	
3.	
4.	
5.	
6.	
7.	
8.	
9.	
10.	

CHAPTER 14

IF IT'S BROKEN, FIX IT

As long as we can tolerate it and get by,
we won't do anything to fix the problem.

It seems obvious. If you have something that's broken, you either fix it or get rid of it and get something that isn't. But, as it goes with duct tape—it's only temporary unless it works—we'll take the easy way and make do if we can. That's as true in the emotional realm as in the physical world.

Have you ever noticed that once you start piling things on a clean desk, countertop or other space, you keep doing it? And before long, you get used to the clutter. Sure, you remember what it was like to have a clean space and how much more room you had. But it would be a lot of work to dig into the pile and actually deal with it, so, you let it go. We do the same thing in our inner world.

Shock Therapy

When we get depressed, the new American way is to run to the doctor for a pill to fix it or otherwise medicate it away. As of the publication of this book, the latest Centers for Disease Control and Prevention statistics say that one in ten Americans takes antidepressants. Now, when I first heard that, I didn't think it could possibly be correct—and not because I thought it was overstating the problem. However, after I read the fine print, the reality was even worse: One in ten Americans *over the age of twelve* takes antidepressants.

Let that sink in for a moment. One in ten people in the US—including children twelve and older—takes pills so they won't be depressed.

Now, there are certainly people included in those studies who are struggling with illness or who are using medication as a temporary measure as they work through traumas. Those are different matters entirely—and not at all what I'm talking about here. I'm talking about people who take pills because they don't want to feel bad—or figure out why they do. I'm talking about people who take pills to help them pretend there's nothing wrong in their lives so they don't have to make changes. *I'm talking about people who take pills instead of responsibility.*

The bottom-line, tough-love truth is that pills do not fix problems—they only dull your pain so you can tolerate what's causing it.

Yes, I know my words are harsh and I know I've pushed a lot of buttons, but it's necessary—it's a message we all need to hear. If we are using anything—drugs (prescription, street or otherwise), alcohol, sex, shopping, fishing, decorating, sports, television, porn, social media, home shopping networks or knitting—to avoid dealing with what we know we need to, it's time to admit it, face it and make different choices. Dulling the pain so we can keep doing what's causing it is insane.

When I was very young, maybe three or four, I was playing with my dolls under the light of the lamp by the front door (exceptional detail to memory for someone who remembers next to nothing about her childhood, but you'll see why). For reasons known only to Little Me, I decided the bobby pin I'd stuck in the doll's hair would be equally amusing inserted into the electrical outlet on the wall. Now you know why I remember.

The shock was fast and fierce. It made a believer out of me and I never ever wanted to feel like that again. I gathered up my toys and found a new place to play that didn't hurt. And I promise you I never stuck unauthorized items in the wall outlet ever again. I learned about electricity—and life—in a way children today can't, all protected from themselves by covers, caps, traps and all manner of devices.

Yes, I suppose I could have been killed, and if I'd done it a second time, I deserved to be. Seriously. Because we all know that if it hadn't hurt me bad enough—and scared me enough—the first time, I would have tried it again, either to see the sparks fly or to get the adrenaline jolt. The only worse choice for that scenario would have been for me to take a pill so I could do it again and hang on longer.

Now, I know there are a lot of people struggling and juggling with situations that seem to have no good solutions, and the best they feel they can do is take a pill to keep them going. Maybe that's okay in the short term—maybe—to keep from cracking like an egg. But at what point is it just another avoidance tactic to keep from having to actually face the unpleasantness and make the tough choices? If the situation doesn't change, temporary becomes forever. And is it really worth putting yourself in purgatory—you're not quite dead, but not living either? Are you going to keep going until someone else makes the decision for you or until a health crisis forces your hand?

The sad fact is, as long as we can tolerate it and get by, we won't actually do anything that could make things better for us in the long run. It *is* like medicating yourself (pick your poison) so you can stick the hairpin in the outlet another time.

Whether it's a personal relationship, a situation at work or simply something we know we need to deal with but don't, the longer we let it go, the harder it is to do what we need to do. We each put on our own particular brand of rose-colored glasses to make it easier to live with what we don't want to face. And before you even realize it, denial, delusion and procrastination become habits—even a way of life.

The Taillight Story

I used to be the undisputed Queen of Denial. I was good, excellent even. When my husband and I divorced, most people were absolutely shocked. Not one person ever said, "Oh, we knew something was wrong." Nope. No one had any idea that all was not well in Happy Valley. We had "looked" like the perfect couple, living the perfect family life—I'd made sure of that. No matter what the *real* situation was, I convinced myself that it wasn't. I rationalized and justified, taking the small bits of truth I could live with and putting a chirpy spin on them. I slapped on a couple of rolls of emotional duct tape and made myself believe the stories I'd concocted so I could tell them convincingly to everyone else.

That creative storytelling skill served me well in the fiction-writing department, but not so well in the real world. Unlike in a novel, where you can control everything, in real life the truth will catch up to you sooner or later. There *will* be a reckoning. There certainly was for me.

After my divorce, I changed the script a little, but I was still writing fiction when I leaped headlong into the relationship with Rebound Guy and wound up in Arkansas. Let's be clear. No one lured me, forced me or otherwise insisted that I do what I did. I did it all by choice—conscious choice fueled by subconscious beliefs, but choice nonetheless. My friends thought I had lost my mind and urged caution, but I wouldn't listen. *I knew what I was doing!*

Obviously, I didn't, and I wound up so far down mentally, emotionally, physically and financially that I still can't believe it. I stayed there for a long time, living in places and circumstances that were beyond my imagination—and not in a good way.

Denial and delusion were still my best friends, and I worked overtime to squash down the feeling that something was wrong—really, really wrong. No matter how my new partner let me down or caused me pain, I always found a loophole for why I shouldn't be angry about it or feel hurt. His actions seemed reasonable and logical, so the problem had to be me. Forget walking on eggshells, I was perched on the edge of a razor blade.

One evening, I was driving Rebound Guy home after he'd injured himself on a job. He'd gone to do some work for an old girlfriend and her husband instead of attending a business dinner with me as he had promised (not kidding, and it was a common occurrence). The typical emotions of betrayal, sympathy, anger, guilt and self-disgust were running me through the proverbial wringer yet again. I was as cold and dark inside as it was outside that night, churning and wrestling with the same old feelings and fears.

I clutched the steering wheel, trying to talk myself out of my anger and despair, trying to justify and rationalize away my feelings. All of a sudden, a car zoomed up behind me and blue lights started flashing. No! My stomach turned another flip and all my emotions rushed to the surface. What now? My whole body was shaking by the time the trooper walked up to the window. I'd been scared, angry and on the verge of tears before I was pulled over. Now, I was teetering on the edge of meltdown.

As the trooper looked over my paperwork, I swallowed the emotions lodged in my throat and tried to keep my teeth from chattering. He asked me if I knew that my taillight was broken. I said yes, I knew, and that, yes, I was aware that it had red tape on it. I explained that I had done that so that it would be okay until I could get it fixed properly. What I didn't say was that it had been broken ever since I had gotten the car—I bought it that way. I also didn't tell him that I hadn't taken it to be fixed because I was afraid of what it would cost to make things right. I believed it was more than I could handle, so I'd ignored it. The tape came loose from time to time, but I always retaped it and made do.

The trooper asked me to step out and walk with him to the back of the car to view the taillight. I did not see why that was necessary and I tried my best to talk him out of it. There was no argument about whether or not the lens was broken—we both agreed it was. We both knew that I'd put tape over it, and apparently some of the tape had come loose. No further discussion was needed—just write the damn ticket and stop the pain! But no, he insisted I get out of the car and go with him so we could look at the situation together.

At the back of the car, I was still shaking like a leaf, shivering from the cold as well as distress, and staring at the stupid broken taillight.

Somehow, though, I was also outside the situation, observing, like in a dream. I was me, but I could also see me. It was a surreal moment.

He looked at me, then pointed to the car. "Do you see that the taillight is broken?"

"Yes, of course," I said, hugging my arms against me to try to stay warm.

"It's broken and you need to fix it."

"Yes, I know, but I put the red tape over it until I could."

He pointed again. "Do you see where this white light is shining through?"

A tiny—and I mean tiny—sliver of light showed through where one edge of the tape had peeled back. "Yes, but I can fix that. I have more tape in the glove box. If you'll just let me get it, I'll fix it right now, and then the light won't shine through. Won't that be okay?"

"Ma'am, the taillight is broken," he repeated, as if talking to a three-year-old. "A piece of tape will not fix it. The light is broken. You have to replace it. You have to get one that is not broken and that works properly. Do you understand?"

God help me, I did, and we were not talking about the taillight. It was a much bigger message he was delivering. I bought a new light the next day. Unfortunately, it took me much longer to fix what I needed to inside the car.

It was so hard to make myself see the truth about that relationship, just as it had been to see the truth of my marriage before it. Both had caused me untold pain, but I wouldn't let go. I couldn't stand to even think of letting go. I begged for help. I swore I would do anything, absolutely anything, to fix the twisted emotional wreck my life had become. I was willing to do anything—except let go of the cause of my pain. Just like the taillight, I knew my relationship was broken, but I was terrified of what dealing with it would cost me.

Eventually, I fixed the taillight, along with the rest of the car. The pain of not doing it finally overcame my fear of what it would cost, and I did what I needed to do. And it didn't cost me nearly as much as I had feared it would—less than a third, in fact. The pain of not dealing with it had been far worse than just doing what I needed to.

The situation regarding the man inside the car worked the same way. When the pain of not facing the truth finally became greater than my fear of what it would cost me if I did, I took action. And yes, exactly what I feared would happen did happen—he didn't want to be around me. Once I finally started respecting myself and acted accordingly, it was over. It had to be. When I stopped running the old script, I couldn't keep saying the old lines, because I had new ones that empowered me. I couldn't play on that same old stage, because I could no longer squeeze myself down small enough to fit it. I had effectively written myself out of that drama and out of the lives of the people still living it. And it was a very good thing.

When we ignore the fact that something is wrong or is hurting us, we are not being respectful of ourselves. People who love and respect themselves do not allow themselves to accept the unacceptable. They fix what needs fixing in the best ways they can.

Please, if you know something in your life is broken, love and respect yourself enough to fix it. Don't keep slapping on a piece of tape and making do. You're only delaying the inevitable, and at some point, there will be a reckoning. The trooper gave me a warning ticket that night, and I carried it in my billfold for a long time as a reminder of what I needed to do. Still, I dragged my feet. You don't have to. Don't wait until you're forced—by circumstances or because a health crisis forces your hand—do what you know you need to do *now*.

Choices, Traps, Distractions and Diversions

As I touched on earlier, my choices in life put me in a position of having very few viable options for leaving my husband. My therapist at the time said, "Wow, you set your trap really well." And I had. With three children two years apart, no degree and zero work experience, exactly what were my options? Without realizing it, I had systematically created an escape-proof situation tailor-made to please my subconscious programming: now, I *had* to be married.

Well, in hindsight, I had far more choices than I believed I did at the time. I also had a lifetime of fears—programmed and self-inflicted—that I wasn't ready to face. I believed that my husband, whom I professed to be my soul mate, would never sell the fancy home in the mountains because it was his dream. He would do whatever it took to keep *that*. I also believed he wouldn't help me and the kids financially. (Side note: Isn't it crazy how we'll stay with people even when we know their true nature? How many times have you heard someone say they're staying married because their spouse would "take everything" if they didn't? Think about what that says about the person you're married to—and yourself!)

Anyway, people told me he would have to sell the house and pay child support, and he would have—eventually. But what was I supposed to do in the meantime? In the end, I wasn't strong enough to leave him and face the world alone. So, instead, I opted to stay and shifted my attention to building an addition on the house and writing a book. I created distractions and diversions to give me something to think about other than the reality I had created for myself. I made the decision to ignore what was broken and focused on something new and interesting instead.

I'm not saying what I did was right or wrong—it just *was*. It was the best I was capable of doing with the awareness and understanding I had at the time. The same goes for you. You can only do what you *can do* when you're ready to do it. That's why you're reading this, and that's why I wrote it for you—to help you see options and possibilities that you might not otherwise. And yes, to push you in the direction you already know you need to go—toward what brings you joy.

TRANSFORMATION INSIGHT

1. If you were pulled over by a trooper right now and had to step outside your car—your life—and view things as an observer, what would you see? Describe it. Describe what's broken that you need to fix.

2. Why haven't you fixed it? What's your fear?

3. What "red tape" have you been using to get by?

4. What action do you need to take so you don't have to keep using your version of red tape?

5. How do you feel when you consider taking action to fix the situation? Describe it in detail.

6. What is one thing—mentally, emotionally or physically—that you can do today that will move you toward fixing your situation? (Is there a phone call you could make? Something you could check on?) Describe what you can think of to do in detail.

7. How would taking that step make you feel right now? Why?

8. How will you feel if you don't? Why?

9. If you don't take that step today, what will help you take it tomorrow? What would make you want to?

10. What would make you not want to? What are you afraid will happen if you do?

CHAPTER 15

IT'S OKAY, I FORGIVE YOU

When you carry around resentment and anger over past wrongs,
the person who hurt you isn't feeling a thing—only you are.

For some of us, acceptance and forgiveness are difficult concepts to get a handle on, primarily because much of what we've been taught is so confusing. Should we favor "eye for an eye" justice or "turn the other cheek"? Should we confront and demand or excuse and let it go? What does it really mean to forgive?

Here are a few statements about accepting and forgiving that you might have heard at one time or another. Which ones do you think are true?

QUIZ I: True or False?

1.	☐ T	☐ F	Acceptance means realizing you just have to put up with things the way they are.
2.	☐ T	☐ F	Accepting that another person has a different opinion means you agree with it.
3.	☐ T	☐ F	Accepting that someone's idea is right means yours has to be wrong.
4.	☐ T	☐ F	Accepting people the way they are means you have to be okay with however they treat you because it's just their way.
5.	☐ T	☐ F	Forgiving means you know the person didn't intend to hurt you and that he or she won't do it again.

6.	☐ T	☐ F	Forgiving means you pretend it never happened and go on the same way you did before.
7.	☐ T	☐ F	Forgiving someone is about taking the high road and showing the person who hurt you, as well as everyone else, that you're the better person.
8.	☐ T	☐ F	.If you forgive someone, it means you have to give him another chance.

ANSWER KEY: 1: False, 2: False, 3. False . . .

Exactly. None of these are true!

First of all, forgiving someone doesn't make you a saint and neither does "accepting people for who they are." You don't get any gold stars in your crown for being a martyr and taking what people dish out just because it's "the way they are."

Second, pretending is lying and that never works out well for anyone. To quote a line from a Jimmy Buffett song: "Live a lie and you will live to regret it." You may find it hard to speak your truth at first, but it will eventually set you free, and you will never go back to accepting anything less.

So, if you are accepting and forgiving and letting bygones be bygones because you think that's what good people do, think again. True acceptance and forgiveness have nothing to do with being good and everything to do with having self-respect.

Now, try these statements:

QUIZ II: True or False?

1.	☐ T	☐ F	You have to accept what you cannot change.
2.	☐ T	☐ F	Acceptance means the conscious acknowledgement of reality.
3.	☐ T	☐ F	When you accept someone as he is, you don't try to change him to be who you want him to be and you don't pretend he's someone he isn't.
4.	☐ T	☐ F	When you accept the reality of a person or a situation, you also accept responsibility for how you respond to him, her or it.
5.	☐ T	☐ F	Acceptance means recognizing what you have control over, what you want in your life and what you don't, then acting accordingly.

6.	☐ T	☐ F	Forgiving means that you acknowledge what occurred and you let go of your attachment to it.
7.	☐ T	☐ F	Forgiving does not mean condoning.
8.	☐ T	☐ F	When you forgive someone, you release your need to carry a grudge for what he or she did "to you."
9.	☐ T	☐ F	Forgiving does not mean that you have to allow a person to hurt you again.
10.	☐ T	☐ F	Forgiving someone is about you.

Yes, they are all true.

The Hurt That Keeps On Hurting

What's also true is that when we hold on to old hurts and resentments, we pay a price. Think of how we express our feelings about these things: *that burns me up; it turns my stomach; that breaks my heart; it makes my blood boil.* And it does. We do get "hot under the collar" when we think about how we've been wronged. Things we think about do make us sick to our stomachs. But did anything really happen to cause it? No, it was just our own thinking that created the feelings for us.

When you keep old wounds open, they are never far from your conscious thoughts, and it doesn't take much to trigger them. Once you start thinking about an old drama, it's as though the whole thing is happening all over again, and you experience the same emotions and physical responses that you did when the original events actually occurred.

The person may have hurt you only once, but *you* hurt yourself every time you replay what "he did to you." When you carry around resentment and anger over past wrongs, the person who hurt you isn't feeling a thing—only you are. By getting angry and reliving old dramas and keeping the pain alive, you're constantly re-experiencing the angst, anxiety and emotional turmoil as if they were still real. You are only hurting *you.*

So, how do you get out of the cycle? What do you do? How do you *not* think about it?

Things to Do

Forgiving isn't about making other people feel okay or be okay or about absolving them of wrongdoing. Forgiving is about cleaning *your* slate and keeping it clean. Here are some things to do that can help put your focus back where it needs to be—on you and your happiness.

1. Serenity Prayer: The opening lines to this prayer, published in the early 1940s by Reinhold Niebuhr, are well known. I know them by heart, and yet I often need to be reminded that I know.

> *God, grant me the serenity to accept the things I cannot change,*
> *Courage to change the things I can,*
> *And wisdom to know the difference.*

2. Face the Facts: Acknowledge that the situation occurred and you were hurt by it.

Dig a little deeper into what the incident triggered for you. Did you feel betrayed or cheated? Did you feel stupid because of what happened? Worthless? What did the person who hurt you take from you? What did you lose? Let yourself explore what you really felt, because this is another great opportunity to uncover some of those underlying beliefs we talked about earlier.

Now, accept that it happened and that you cannot change it. Acknowledge that it's over, that it is in the past and that the only place it exists now is in your mind.

3. Play Gotcha: When you notice an old thought pattern coming in, stop it and say a standard phrase to yourself. It can be anything that works for you, but here are some ideas: "Stop! The past is past. I live in the now and I am happy!" Or, maybe, "Ha, I caught you! Now, back to the past where you belong. I am free and happy, and I live in joy!" You can try "I release it, I release it, I release it. I now live in joy." Find something that works for you and use it every single time you catch the old thoughts slipping in.

You'll be amazed at how quickly the old ways of thinking and feeling can disappear when you police your thoughts. Then, when someone brings up the situation or something makes you think of it, you won't have the emotional ties to it anymore. It will be as unemotional as talking about watching grass grow. It's just something that happened that has no bearing on who you are or how you feel today. You can say, "Yeah, I remember that" and then easily dismiss it, move on to another thought and stay in your joy.

4. Tune Your Surround Sound: It is much easier to stay in a good place when you're surrounded with positive thoughts, materials and people, so make a conscious effort to monitor the influences you're choosing. What you watch on TV, what you read, what music you listen to, what conversations you engage in and what you tell yourself in your head all affect how you feel and think and what you do. The old "garbage in, garbage out" adage holds true. Put in good stuff and you'll have good stuff to work with—and good stuff will come out.

Magical Thinking

Okay, now that you've made peace with yourself and you're in a positive place, does that mean that things go back to the way they were before with that person?

Absolutely not. Things can never be the same. And why would you want them to be? If things are the same, then the same things will happen all over again—that's the definition of "the same."

Here's a great way to set yourself up for future unpleasant déjà vu moments: "Oh, I know she didn't really mean it. I've forgiven her and I know she won't do it again."

First of all, it's a lie. When you say that sort of thing, what you're really saying is that you're going to pretend nothing happened and that you weren't hurt by it so that you don't have to deal with the real issues. You haven't forgiven a thing, You're just agreeing not to face the problem directly, hoping that somehow it will all magically be okay. You're deluding yourself with the notion that, because you are such an understanding and forgiving soul, she has automatically realized how she's wronged you and has been miraculously transformed to treat you better in the future.

Has that *ever* happened?

Just because you've changed your way of looking at the world and dealing with things doesn't mean that anyone else has. People don't change their nature just because you want it to be true. Besides, the person may see the situation totally differently and think *you* are the one who wronged *her*.

Acceptance means that you deal with reality and you take responsibility for your own feelings and how you allow people to treat you. When you have a problem, you address the situation directly and openly. You calmly state how you perceived what occurred, how you felt about it and what you would like to do to resolve it. In short, you act like an adult and use emotional maturity.

You don't just say, "Oh, it's okay, I know you didn't mean it." You put on your big-kid pants and tell the person what he or she did, why it's unacceptable and what you're going to do about it. That way, there is no confusion, no need for behind-the-scenes drama and no worries on your part about having to deal with a similar situation again.

Yes, it could mean that the person may never speak to you again. If so, I ask you, what's wrong with that? Why do you want a "friend" who causes you pain and who you can't be yourself with? Why do you want to hang around someone who can't be honest and isn't willing to take personal responsibility for her actions? Is that really what you need in your life?

Outcomes

Sometimes, no matter what you do, the new you just doesn't fit in the old dynamic of a relationship. If the other person is attached to things being as they always have, you have to accept it and allow it to be what it is. You can still love the person, even if things are a bit different, but it may mean that you won't be seeing each other as much—or maybe at all.

If you do stay in contact, however, it won't affect you in the same ways it did. You're over what happened and it no longer holds any power over how you think or feel or what you do. You aren't walking on eggshells anymore, trying to make things okay. Things are okay for you. And if the other person tries to dredge up the old drama—or create a new one—you'll be able to address it immediately and matter-of-factly, unattached to the outcome.

There's always the possibility, of course, that the person will appreciate your new straightforward manner and the relationship will be better and stronger because of it. I hope so! Two people can come out of a bad situation much stronger and healthier for it if they are both willing to be honest, take responsibility and make a conscious commitment to do differently.

Whatever the case, once you have forgiven the past, you no longer need an apology or acknowledgment of the wrong done to you— you're okay regardless. You have taken responsibility for your own feelings and choices and freed yourself of all the old hurts. You are now living your life on your terms, and the only person you need approval from is yourself.

TRANSFORMATION INSIGHT 15

For the next questions, answer them as if you hadn't read this chapter. Allow yourself to answer with every petty, spiteful or angry thought that you've ever had about the situations in question. Be childish, be mean, be whatever it takes to get all the ugly stuff out in the open. You can't clean out the septic tank without taking off the lid, so, crawl into the muck and get to it!

In this first section, list three people who have wronged you. Describe what they did and how it made you feel. Describe what each of those people could do to fix the situation and how you would feel if they did. Can you ask them to do what you describe? Why or why not?

Who	What happened, how they wronged you, how you felt	What could they do to right the wrong?	How you'd feel	Possible? Why/why not?
1.				
2.				
3.				

In the next section, list three people who owe you something and explain why. Describe how you feel about it. Describe what they could do to pay you back and how it would feel if they did. Can you ask them to pay you back? Why or why not?

Who	What happened, what they owe you, how you feel	What could they do to repay or clear the debt?	How you'd feel	Possible? Why/why not?
1.				
2.				
3.				

1. Think of a situation where you had a falling out with someone. Describe what happened.

2. How was the situation resolved? If it wasn't, what prevented it?

3. What have you not forgiven that person for?

4. What have you not forgiven yourself for?

5. What would it take to feel peaceful about the situation and the person?

6. What's preventing that?

1. Think of a situation where you feel stuck, where someone else is keeping you from having what you want. Describe the situation; explain what the person is doing and how it's holding you back.

2. If that person weren't holding you back, what could you be doing? What actions would you be free to take?

3. How would taking those steps get you what you want?

4. Are there any actions on that list that you could take now? Why or why not?

CHAPTER 16

TALK ISN'T CHEAP

---

*There's a high price to pay for lying to yourself,
and your health is one of the currencies.*

It's true that talk is cheap and it's what you *do* that really counts. But, when the talking is unconsciously controlling the doing, it can cost you—big time—and in ways you may not have ever considered.

We've already touched on how we talk about our old wounds, how things make our "blood boil" or make us "sick to our stomachs." This chapter expands on those thoughts and explores the connections between our thoughts, emotions and physical symptoms. Yes, the mind-body connection.

Identity Crisis

A lot of people are very attached to their physical ailments—it's who they are. Their physical problems are their personal identities and their whole vocabularies revolve around them.

Once, at a school function, a woman asked me which child was mine. I answered and pointed. She pointed out her daughter and noted that she had to keep a close eye on her because she had asthma. Within seconds, the woman had given me the child's complete medical history and associated pharmaceuticals list, along with what she could and couldn't do because of it. She also informed me that *every-one* in her family had it, even the youngest child, who actually didn't have it yet, but would because everyone in her family got it. I was truly stunned. I think all I said was, "Wow."

A man I once worked with couldn't tell a story about what happened the evening before without including his routine for checking his blood sugar, giving himself his insulin shot, determining how much orange juice he had to drink and how weak he felt before, during and after, and so on. I never knew if he was looking for sympathy or pity, or if it made him feel special because he had to do all those things. All I know is that it made him appear weak and needy, and that had nothing at all to do with the fact that he had diabetes.

Now, I am not in any way minimizing or trivializing health issues. I am simply pointing out that we can have significant attachments to them and probably not even realize it. Take me, for example...

That's Not the Problem

When I was about thirty-two, I was convinced that I was in menopause. Yes, really. I had *all* the signs. I had done extensive research, and the symptoms I was experiencing matched my diagnosis step for step—I had proof.

I dutifully went to the doctor, explained my situation, then waited patiently for her to applaud me for my brilliant diagnostic assessment and tell me how she was going to fix things. Needless to say, things did not go according to plan. The doctor told me that it was highly unlikely that I was in menopause at age thirty-two. Then she started asking questions to try to figure out what was going on. I don't remember what all she asked because I quit listening when she didn't tell me what I wanted to hear. However, I was still convinced my diagnosis was correct. Since I probably looked ready to combust, she agreed to do some blood work to pacify me and told me to come back in a few weeks.

When I went back to get the test results, she started asking more questions, and I did not like the way things were going. She got very serious and told me that I was not in menopause, nor was I in any pre-stage thereof—or even remotely close to it. What I was, she told me, was unhappy in my marriage. What? How dare she suggest such a thing! She didn't even know me! She said that the questions she had been asking me—sneaking in on me—told her that I had problems in my relationship, and that they were serious, and I needed to address those with a therapist. The only thing that she, as a physician, could do for me was prescribe an antidepressant. Well, I hit the roof! I most certainly did *not* need a therapist, and I would *not* be taking any drugs, thank you very much. And how *dare* she suggest that there could be anything at all wrong in Happy Valley!

But there was.

Since I didn't get any help from the doctor, I took care of things myself. I loaded up on sam-E and St. John's wort for my "moods" and took an antihistamine so that I could sleep at night. I also took a high-octane anti-reflux pill so that in my semi-comatose state I didn't choke to death on the bile lurching up into my throat. I kept a bottle of antacids at my side 24/7 and snacked on them like candy. There's probably more, that's just what I remember.

Then, one day, something I had tolerated a thousand times before was no longer tolerable and I snapped. I spontaneously blurted out that I wanted a divorce. I was as shocked as he was, but I didn't take it back—nor did he ask me to. I had *finally* become willing to see the truth of what my life had become and acknowledge that I had to change it.

Once the house sold, my husband made his semi-permanent home on the other side of the world permanent and I moved to another state with the kids. Then something strange happened. I quit buying antacid tablets because my stomach had stopped spewing acid into my throat. I fell asleep without even thinking about whether I needed to take anything or not—and I slept well. I kept forgetting to take my "mood" pills, but I felt great, happy even. It was a miracle!

No, it was a textbook case of the mind-body connection. My body had been giving me signal after signal that things were wrong. When I found peace, so did my body.

You Are What You Say

During those dark times—the ones before my divorce and those that came not long after—my words reflected my truth. I often said that I was a "nervous wreck," that I was "sick of it" and that it "made me want to vomit." And so it was. When the situation no longer made me sick, I wasn't.

We've all seen this happen, of course. Even our everyday language tells us that emotional distress creates physical distress. How often do we hear people say things like:

> *He's such a pain in the neck*
> *That just turns my stomach*
> *He's eaten up with guilt*
> *It was like a kick to the gut*
> *That just burns my butt*
> *This is killing me*
> *It just breaks my heart*
> *I am so sick and tired of . . .*

Just as it had when my marriage needed to end, my wonderful body did its job, getting my attention with similar messages about how things were not right in the relationship with Rebound Guy. The menopause thing hadn't worked out so well before, so this time I didn't try to find a physical excuse for my symptoms. I knew that the reason I felt bad was emotional and that I needed to do something different. So, I decided to take the bull by the horns and fix what was wrong—me. As you know, I made everything that was wrong in the relationship my fault. If I was to blame, then all I had to do was fix me, which would in turn fix the relationship. Then things would be better, I would feel better and all would be right with the world.

This plan worked about as well as it sounds like it would. I put all my effort into it, analyzing and twisting things until I thought I had my every flaw uncovered. I worked hard not to do anything "wrong," but things didn't get better, and I just felt worse and worse. Several times a day, for seemingly trivial reasons, I would get this zinging, cutting feeling that started in my groin and shot all the way up to my throat. I said it made me feel as if I was being gutted like a fish—ripped open with my whole insides exposed. Half the time I couldn't eat, my stomach was always gurgling, I had heart palpitations and I coughed continuously. At one point, I was so sick I really thought I might die.

To use my own language at the time, I was "turning myself inside out" to salvage the relationship. He "broke my heart" so many times that I wasn't even sure I had one left. No matter how good his excuses, it often felt like he was lying about something and I was "sick to my stomach" over worrying what it might be. I didn't have what I really wanted, but I wasn't ready to "cough up" the truth that if I stayed with him, I never would. I was going to fix things or die trying.

Looking back on it now, it all seems so foolish. But emotions are not foolish, they just *are*, and they are very powerful. And when we don't understand what's really going on—what underlying beliefs and motivations are driving us—we fight against ourselves and we get sick.

The Body's a Snitch

Feeling bad is a signal from your body that you have a problem. That problem may be mental, emotional, physical or, most likely, all three. You might run and hide from it for a while, but eventually your body *will* rat you out.

Below are a few common physical issues and emotional connections. As you read through them, think about people you know, then see if you can connect the dots between their stresses and their physical conditions.

1. Backs, Necks and Shoulders: Backaches are wonderful sources of insight into what is going on in our minds. Notice how we talk about getting a "catch" in our backs or our backs being "out." Back pain reflects what we carry around with us, the burdens of life, our fears and worries. Anxiety over finances, for example, can show up as lower back pain.

Neck pain can be an easy one to trace. Who or what is a pain in the neck for you? When do you notice your neck feeling stiff? What's going on? Where are you? What are you thinking about? While I was working at one company, my neck became so stiff that I could barely move it. When I tried, it crunched like it was full of gravel, and I walked around with it cocked to the side to try to ease the pain. When that job ended, so did my neck problems.

Shoulders are fairly obvious. Does it feel like you're carrying the weight of the world on your shoulders? Are you slumped over in defeat from it? Or are you standing tall, shoulders back, handling whatever comes with optimism?

2. Colds, Flu and Mental Sniffles: Many people consider colds and flu to be "common" and "unavoidable." They aren't. Many people never get sick, regardless of who or what they're exposed to. However, people who believe they get whatever's "going around"—those who swear they *always* get three colds each year or get sick when the weather changes—do. They are always right. Some are even kind of proud of their prophetic abilities.

Are you one of the plan-ahead types? If you plan on being sick, ask yourself why. What do you get out of it? What is it you're really wanting, and why do you need to be sick to get it?

A lot of people resist this kind of thinking, but give it a chance. You may learn some interesting things about yourself and find better ways to give yourself what you really need.

3. Head Games: Headaches can stem from a variety of sources. Look at the language you use to describe it. Does it feel like your head is about to explode? What's pounding on your mind? What thought wants your attention? What's the source of the pressure that makes your head feel like it's splitting open?

4. Reproductivity: Reproductive organs can be affected when we face issues that bring up feelings about our gender and gender roles.

For men, work changes due to health issues, layoffs, termination or retirement can trigger impotence or problems with the prostate or testicles. For women, anxieties about having or not having children can manifest in obvious ways as well. Breasts are associated with nurturing, but are you nurturing *yourself?*

5. Downtime: Stress compromises the immune system and all other systems, so when you've pushed too hard and just need a break, your body makes you take one. Being sick gives you an acceptable reason to check out for a while. If you're too sick to get out of bed—you're too sick to move or think—your body and mind get the rest they need by default. So, if you need downtime, don't wait until you're forced to take it—and have to feel miserable to justify it. Own your needs. Take the time off to rest and relax. Do it on purpose and enjoy it!

6. Mind-Body Connect-the-Dots: In most situations, the functions of the body and feelings are easy to figure out. Feet are our foundation and get us where we need to go. So, if your feet hurt or "get knocked out from under you," you may not feel your life is on solid ground or moving forward. Teeth grind—what are you chewing on? Knees bend—or don't—what are you unwilling to be flexible about? There are many specifics and nuances, of course, but you get the idea. Louise Hay's wonderful book *You Can Heal Your Life* makes it easy to understand how thoughts and emotions manifest in the body and how they can be managed for healing. I *strongly* recommend you read it.

Talking Trash

"No, really, it's okay. Everything's fine. I'm happy." Saying something that isn't true over and over doesn't make it become true. You may be trying to convince everyone you're as happy as a clam, but your body knows different. That kind of talk *is* cheap. It's not so cheap when you're vowing how something makes you sick. Either way, your body

knows the truth—*you* know the truth—and it *will* catch up with you. There's a high price to pay for lying to yourself, and your health is one of the currencies.

TRANSFORMATION INSIGHT 16

Now that you have some examples of how our bodies talk to us, can you see some mind-body connections in your own life?

List five beliefs you have about your health.

1.

2.

3.

4.

5.

What are the health problems that run in your family?

1.

2.

3.

4.

5.

What words or phrases that refer to your body do you say without really thinking about it (I never get sick, that makes me sick, etc.)?
1.
2.
3.
4.
5.

List health conditions you have that require treatment, as well as the areas of your body where you hurt.	For each, describe what causes or worsens the condition, as well as what triggers any pain.	For each, describe what makes it better.	Describe the times and situations when you have the most or least discomfort (e.g., neck may be stiff at work).
1.			
2.			

List health conditions you have that require treatment, as well as the areas of your body where you hurt.	For each, describe what causes or worsens the condition, as well as what triggers any pain.	For each, describe what makes it better.	Describe the times and situations when you have the most or least discomfort (e.g., neck may be stiff at work).
3.			
4.			
5.			

CHAPTER 17

HEALTHY CHOICES

If what you really want is to be healthy, but you love being lazy and eating unhealthy foods, something's gotta give.

In the last Transformation Insight, you identified your beliefs about health, the vocabulary you use and the specific health issues you're dealing with. So, I'm guessing that you, like me, might have a few things you want to take a closer look at in the health and fitness realm. Well, as with anything, the best place to start is with the basics.

Life Essentials

We all know we need to drink water, eat good food, get plenty of rest and exercise, so it might seem silly to list them here. It's not. Without those four things, you simply can't be healthy. And you might not be doing quite as well with all of them as you think you are—I certainly wasn't. When I started looking into things, I was surprised by what I found. So, read on. You might be surprised too.

1. Sleep—new reasons to get more: It sounds obvious, but how many of us really get the amount of deep sleep that we need? Many of us don't routinely, and it shows. Without an adequate amount of the deep sleep we need, and without adequate time to rejuvenate each night, our bodies can't perform at optimal levels. We may feel tired all the time, look haggard, suffer from fuzzy thinking and experience lowered libido. You probably know all that, but did you know that lack of sleep can also be a factor in weight gain?

Recent studies show that not getting enough sleep affects the body's production of chemicals that control appetite and hunger sensations and, consequently, contribute to weight gain. Leptin, which is produced when we get adequate sleep, is an appetite suppressant and keeps us from feeling hungry. So, not getting enough sleep means there's not enough leptin in the system and we feel hungry all the time. That's enough to get our attention, but it's only half of this one-two punch. Lack of sleep also causes an increase in another chemical, ghrelin, that tells our brains we're hungry and need to eat, often causing cravings for carbohydrates.

By not getting the sleep we need, we're actually giving ourselves a double shot of chemicals that will drive us to eat more. And we haven't even touched on the effects of metabolism, eating for comfort and energy, and other issues associated with sleep deprivation.

If you're interested in the science behind these chemical appetite directors, there are several studies, including a recent one at Stanford, that give details. Researchers don't know all there is to know about the interactions of these two chemicals and weight, not by a long shot, but they've given us good motivation for doing what we know we should do anyway—get the good rest we need.

In short, we can distill it all down into two simple equations:

Less than 7 hours of sleep =
look and feel bad + fuzzy thinking + gain weight

More than 7 hours of sleep =
look and feel good + optimal brain function +
natural weight regulation

Now, if you've been getting by on five or six hours of sleep for years, you may be wondering if everyone really needs seven hours of sleep. Or, if you do have lights-out time for seven or more hours, how do you know if you're getting enough of the right kind of sleep?

Well, the truth is, you know. We all know.

For me, the face in the mirror is the best indicator of whether I am honoring my body's need for good sleep—or not—and it's only a glance away. If I ignore the mirror, the second indicator that shows up to get my attention is brain function—I just don't think as clearly as I normally do. I can feel dizzy, off balance and "spacey," among other things. If I let it go too long, well, let's just say I shouldn't be out roaming the streets alone. And I won't be for long, because the next step for me is that my body just shuts down and I have no choice but to sleep—for a long time.

Recently, when I broke my own cardinal rule of not working between the hours of 3 and 5 a.m.—my important biorhythm time—I knew I had crossed the line. So, before my body did it for me, I had an intervention for myself. I slept for over ten hours, regrouped and put myself on a reasonable schedule.

We all have different needs and different internal clocks, and your optimal sleep time is something you're going to have to figure out for yourself. Conduct your own study of how your body responds to various sleep times and durations. Keep a journal of the times, hours and quality of sleep. Record how you feel, level of energy, hunger and so forth, and you should get a pretty good idea of your optimal sleep needs.

Do be mindful of sleeping too much—more than is normal for you—because that can be an indication of a health condition, including depression, that needs to be addressed by a professional.

It also goes without saying that the quality of the sleep is critical. Lying in bed for seven hours but never getting into deep-level sleep—either because of health conditions such as sleep apnea or for situational or emotional reasons—still means you're not getting the sleep you need. If you need to see a doctor or other health professional, see one. If you need to change something about your sleeping place or situation, change it. Adequate sleep is critical to your health and life expectancy.

2. Exercise—flip your mattress, flip your mind: By now you're probably pretty clear that we all have limiting beliefs, and that they call the shots in our lives whether we realize it or not. One that was a big eye-opener for me was about exercise.

Several years ago, a good friend of mine was on a health kick and wanted to walk. I was not keen on the idea. If I was going to expend energy, I wanted something tangible to show for it, such as clean stalls in the barn, a nice stack of hay, a new rock retaining wall or a freshly painted house. Work was my definition of exercise. However, I figured a little fresh air couldn't hurt. And it was supposed to be good for me, right?

Since I had a nice place to walk where I lived, my friend came to my house. When she arrived, I asked her if she'd mind helping me flip my mattress. She said sure, but asked if I wanted to do it before we went for the walk or after.

"Oh, better do it now," I said without hesitation. "Afterward we'll be tired and won't feel like doing *anything*."

As the words left my mouth, a lightbulb went on in my head. I realized that I had just uncovered a serious limiting belief—one I'd had my whole life. I believed that *exercise made me feel bad!* No wonder I never wanted to do anything that could be labeled "exercise." Why would I want to do something I believed was going to make me feel *worse*?

I don't know when or how I came up with that belief—and it doesn't matter. What matters is that I recognized the automatic programming for what it was. My Belief Monkey had popped up with another subconscious limitation that I didn't realize I had, and I knew I could change the belief if I wanted to. So, I laughed at myself and shared my insights with my friend. Then I reworded the belief and tried my response again. "Let's wait until we get back, because after our walk we'll feel great and have more energy than we know what to do with!"

A very different way of viewing things, isn't it? It's also easy to see how operating on that belief system would produce radically different choices and create different outcomes for me than the old one I had. The best part of the whole thing was that I started feeling great! I loved the changes in my body as I got it in better shape, and I loved the changes in my mind even more. Today, I do all kinds of things to keep my body active and love to try new ones. Changing that one limiting belief, one I didn't even know I had, changed everything.

So, what are *your* limiting beliefs? What do you just automatically say as "fact" that may just be an opinion? What offhand comments do you make without really hearing or thinking about them? Start listening to what you say, and you may be amazed at what you discover—and at how simple it can be to make changes because of it.

While we're at it, we need to talk about weight. Pay attention to what you tell yourself about *that*. A lot of people are very attached to hitting a particular weight goal, and if that works for you, fine, but being healthy and in shape isn't about a number. You can hit your target weight and still be very unhealthy, so focus on fitness. How do you feel? How do your clothes fit? What activities can you do?

Seeing yourself healthy, fit and living life to the fullest is a great motivator. So, define what being healthy and in shape means to you, and start living a lifestyle that reflects it. Take the time to get clear on *why* you want to be healthy and fit, and use it as a motivator. What is it you can't do now that you're going to love doing once your body's in shape? Will you be able to go with your family on a hike? Walk up the stairs at the stadium without huffing and puffing? Wear a sexy swimsuit? Learn to ski? Run through the airport to catch a flight to Venice? Whatever it is, focus on *that*. See yourself living that goal and you'll automatically make wise health choices to create it. You'll want to exercise because you're focused on the payoff. And before long, you won't even think of it as exercise at all, but just what you do and who you are—the fit, healthy and fabulous you who can do all the things you've always wanted to!

3. Water—how much do you really drink? You know how important it is to keep a constant supply of clean water flowing through your body. It keeps you hydrated, flushes out toxins, rebuilds cells, keeps your kidneys happy, eases headaches and helps your mind stay clear and focused. So, how much is enough?

As with most things, it varies by individual according to gender, body size, activity level and other factors. For most of us, just drinking when we're thirsty probably won't give us the amount of water that our bodies need. If your urine is a dark yellow, you're definitely not getting enough water.

The old standard of eight eight-ounce glasses a day may be just fine for some. Some *might* even be fine with less. For others, it isn't nearly enough. Someone who is highly active or sweating all day will need more than someone who isn't. Again, it's essential to know your body and figure out what it needs to be at the top of its game.

I used to get highly irritated at my mother over drinking water, or actually the not drinking of water. She had chronic kidney problems, but couldn't see any connection with her anti-water habits—and didn't want to. I explained, begged and nagged, and eventually she agreed to keep a glass by the sink as I do, promising to fill it and drink it every time she went to the bathroom. The idea was to keep one thing triggering the other. It's a simple plan and it works.

Since I lived two states away, her emphatic promises that she was following directions to the letter kept me pacified. And what was I going to do about it anyway, send in the water police eight times a day to check on her? I wish I could have done exactly that, because what she said she'd been doing and what she actually had been weren't even in the same ballpark.

I quickly discovered that "drinking a *big ol' glass* of water *all* the time" translated to taking a few sips from a six-ounce juice glass when it crossed her mind. The only time she even came close to drinking a full glass was when I was staring her down. Obviously, I was fighting a battle I wasn't going to win.

The other day I was out in the heat and, as on many hot days, the water I was drinking wasn't making the full circuit. What I wasn't sweating out was bloating me like a toad. Knowing that one thing to do when you're retaining water is to drink more of it, I did. My body took a lot of convincing, but it eventually started trusting that I'd keep the fluid coming and the cells started releasing their reserves.

During the process, however, I discovered a few things about myself. One was that my perception of how much water I routinely drank and the reality of it were quite different. I always have a cup of herbal or green tea with me and drink water besides—but when I started consciously paying attention to exactly how much, it wasn't anywhere near what I'd thought. In fact, as I stood there measuring the volume of the glass I'd been using, I had a rude awakening—I'd become my mother, complete with a juice glass that I wasn't filling to the top or finishing.

Yes, it sucked to realize that, and it isn't pleasant to admit it here either, but facts are facts. So, I took the various glasses that I typically used and measured how much I usually drank. I averaged about three-quarters of a cup each time. What was my own "big ol' glass of water" in my head was only giving me about 75 percent of what I believed it was—at best. I wasn't nearly the big water drinker I perceived myself to be.

So, before you tell me you're certain you drink plenty of water, prove it to yourself first. If you're someplace where you can, keep a glass and a notepad by the sink for one full day and write down how many glasses of water you drank and how much was in each. If you're on the go, take the notepad with you and do the best you can. Remember, ice takes up a lot of space, so factor that into your estimates. Water bottles with ounce measurements make it easy, but if yours doesn't have that, use a measuring cup to get a feel for the actual volume at various levels.

Once you've spent a day documenting your drinking, you'll know what you're actually doing and can then make conscious choices to do something different if you want to. For me, that meant doing exactly what I'd told my mother to do—drink a full eight ounces every time I go to the bathroom. I can keep drinking my tea, but I can't delude myself that it's enough anymore.

I've heard some people say they hate water and it's a punishment to have to drink it. In those cases, there is only one thing to do—reprogram. You have to change your belief. As long as you believe that water tastes terrible and that you're being punished by having to drink it, you simply won't do it. You can't. Why would you? There's nothing in it for you except pain. So, become willing to change your belief and do some things differently.

First of all, water does have a taste. Get a filter on your faucet, or get a self-filtering pitcher. These use charcoal as a filtering agent and generally eliminate things that cause water to taste bad. Secondly, if drinking water feels like punishment, figure out why. Can you remember when you started hating water? What happened? Yes, a visit to your childhood is probably in order. Don't fight it; just do it. You may even get some insights about other issues.

Now that you're willing to reprogram your beliefs and you may have discovered a reason for them, the next thing to do is find your angle. What motivates you? Do you respond better to carrots or sticks? What's going to get your attention and make you want to change?

Do you want to have better health, feel more energized, have increased longevity, look younger, heal quicker or improve your stamina? Or do you want to stop feeling tired or looking haggard? Do you want to eliminate the medications that not taking care of your body requires? What do you want? Whatever it is, associate it with giving your body what it needs, including water.

Now, many of you may be thinking that you get plenty of water because you drink soda all day long. Well, that's like eating hot-fudge sundaes to get the milk. Just think how hard your body has to work to get what it needs out of water that's been "contaminated" with artificial colors, sweeteners, preservatives, caffeine and other things. Every time you put a soda to your lips, your kidneys and liver shudder, and if they could, they'd scream, "Give me a break!"

I'm not being melodramatic here. What you put into your body matters. The hard truth is either you're willing to do what it takes to have a healthy body, including letting go of things you know are harmful, or you're not. If you're not, suck it up and be honest about it. Admit that you're willing to accept the damage to your body in order to indulge your habits and addictions. Admit that you'd rather complain about feeling bad and keep running to the doctor for repairs and medicine rather than take steps that could help you. Take responsibility. Own your choices and their consequences.

On that happy note, let's talk about food choices.

4. Food—it's healthy for a reason: "You are what you eat" may not be the literal truth, but what you put into your body matters.

I grew up in the South, and what was considered healthy back then and what I consider healthy now are two wildly different things. You can't even begin to talk about Southern cooking without using the words *deep-fried* and *chicken-fried*—both definitely gravy-fied—along with hot buttered biscuits, pecan pie and sweet tea. I know my way around a Southern kitchen and even indulge myself in eating a little comfort food from time to time. However, I know for a fact that I feel better and look better when I don't. And knowing that makes it much easier to make wiser choices on a daily basis.

Whether you were brought up with a deep-fried sweet tooth or you cultivated it later in life, letting go of the addiction (let's call it what it is) can be a challenge. Turning down French fries in favor of fresh, crunchy and colorful salads and lightly steamed vegetables can take some convincing. But if you do, you'll be amazed at the results. You'll feel better and your body will get healthier and leaner naturally, which makes the good food choices even more appealing.

There is an enormous amount of material about eating healthy, and I especially like knowing what foods are helpful for specific health conditions, as well as foods to avoid in certain situations. One book that I've found helpful is Dr. Bernard Jensen's *Foods That Heal*, which gives some easily understandable explanations and lists the therapeutic effects of different foods. If you have a health concern, do some research and find out the best—and worst—foods for your particular situation, then check with your physician first to be sure the dietary changes are appropriate for you. Knowing what you can eat—or not eat—to improve your condition is empowering. Take charge of your health!

Below is a reminder list of things you can do to help get you into the habit of eating healthy, thinking healthy and wanting to *be* healthy. You

know this stuff, but whether or not you do it is another story. And you
don't have to, of course—it's your choice. Just remember, every choice
comes with consequences—good or bad—so, you're also choosing those.

- **Forget fried and fatty foods.** You can drop major calories by
  doing this one thing alone, not to mention that your arteries will
  love you for it. You know it's true, so do it!

- **Shake off sugars and sweeteners.** Most of us eat way too much
  sugar, and obesity and diabetes are rampant. The connections
  are obvious, so start weaning yourself off the sweet stuff. Fake
  sugar isn't the answer either. They weren't all developed as ant
  poison, but they're still chemically created, so make your decisions
  accordingly. Honey and plant-based sweeteners, such as agave and
  stevia, offer options, but require adjustments for baking and other
  uses. Needing fewer "sweet fixes" of any kind is the best option.

- **Can the sodas.** Yes, even diet ones—maybe especially those.
  Your body doesn't need whatever is in either kind. I think
  eliminating soft drinks is one of the easiest ways to lose weight.
  There's something in the stuff besides the empty calories—some
  invisible gremlins—that turn your body into a fat-making
  machine. No, I don't have scientific proof, but that's the belief
  that works for me. Drink herbal teas, natural juices and water—
  lots of it—instead.

- **Back off highly processed foods**, particularly those with white
  flour. Easier said than done, but choosing whole-grain products
  when possible, and cutting down on doughy things in general,
  helps avoid a bunch of calories whose only mission is to make
  you look like a dough ball.

- **Munch more fresh fruits and vegetables**. Sure, you know it,
  but do you actually do it? Vegetables served fresh, steamed,

lightly grilled or stir-fried in healthy, heat-stable oils provide a great source of natural vitamins and minerals, fiber and other essential nutrients. Unlike deep-fried, overcooked or sauce-laden versions, they won't weigh you down or make you feel sluggish. And remember, making "colorful" choices in your foods—leafy greens, luscious reds, bright yellows and vibrant oranges—can help balance your intake of different nutrients naturally.

• **Pick proteins wisely.** We have to be mindful of what our bodies need for optimal function—and what they don't. We need protein in our diets, but how much and what variety are up for debate, and the considerations of steroids, hormones, herbicides, pesticides, heavy metals and genetic modification only add to the confusion. Generally, the experts seem to favor going lighter on red meats and pork and emphasizing fish and chicken, with beans, including soybean tofu, offering good options as well. Whatever your preference, do your own research and always choose the healthiest and freshest options possible. Some stores pack meats in puffed and pressured containers to keep it from turning green and extend shelf life, so check around for fresh, chemical-free options.

• **Come clean about caffeine.** A cup of coffee or glass of tea because you enjoy it is one thing. If you need highly caffeinated drinks in order to function, you have a problem—deal with it.

• **Lose the junk food.** Don't keep temptations around the house. If it isn't there, you won't eat it. Instead, make sure you have plenty of healthy options to nibble on. Start seeing cookies, cakes, donuts, chips, crackers and candy for what they are—feel-good fixes that taste good in the moment and make you feel lousy later. Train your body to crave healthy options, such as fresh fruits, yogurt, rice cakes and such. There are some great snack options available now, but be sure you aren't just buying hype.

Healthy Thinking Basics

That list of dietary dos and don'ts gave pretty clear-cut ways to get your thinking straight about food. Being mindful of what your body is telling you is another great way to create and reinforce positive health beliefs. Take note of how you feel after you eat certain kinds of foods. Do you feel energized or sluggish? Do you have heartburn? Is grease dripping out of your pores? Does it feel like you have a rock in your stomach? Do you feel sleek and satisfied? Something that may taste good in the moment may leave you feeling horrible in a couple of hours. Pay attention to your body's reactions, and you'll have the information you need to help you with the next suggestion.

Form a link in your mind between good foods and feeling and looking good. When deciding what to eat, instead of thinking about how it tastes, think about how it will make you feel and look. If you like the outcome, go for it. If you don't, make a different choice. It is easy to walk away from a donut when you have a clear picture of what it's going to look like on your stomach and you know how you're going to feel in an hour or so. Reaching for an apple, a cup of yogurt, or another healthy choice is easier when you know you'll feel good and look good because of it.

Learn to read your body's signals and hear what it wants. This can take a bit of practice, since you may initially be distracted by a voice screaming that it wants cake, donuts and ice cream. But once you develop a solid link between knowing what is good for your body and being willing to choose it, your body will start giving you specifics.

Because I trust my body to tell me what it needs, I don't stress over food. If it "calls to me," I eat it. I never deprive myself of anything. I frequent Chinese buffets a lot, and many times, I eat the same things, but I don't do it out of habit. I just eat what sounds good at that particular time. There are times when I've craved tomatoes, pickled ginger, bananas or even gelatin. There are times when I want nothing but shrimp or crab legs. Whatever it is, I go with it.

For several weeks, I found myself eating a lot of sweet potatoes. As it turned out, stress had triggered a physical issue for me, and when I looked up what to do about it, one of the primary things to eat was sweet potatoes. My body had already known what it needed. That sort of thing happened a lot for me when I was pregnant too. I remember eating cans of whole peeled tomatoes—and hiding the fact from my husband so he wouldn't make fun of me.

Now, I openly honor what I want. Yes, some days that includes sweets. Other days, it's guacamole and cottage cheese. I don't eat things just because they're there; I eat what my body needs and wants. This system works for me because I know my body will tell me what it needs and that I will feel good because of it.

The same thing goes with exercise. Your body will tell you what it needs in the fitness department too, if you'll really listen. Pain is the body's way of telling you something isn't right. But feeling stiff after sitting isn't a message to sit back down. To feel good and move freely, you have to move *more*. Just like the Tin Man, if you don't keep moving, you rust—and not just in your joints. *Not* doing creates all kinds of complications—physical and mental.

I was in the grocery store the other day and heard a woman talking on the phone, bemoaning how horrible she felt. "I don't know who said life starts at fifty," she grumbled. "Well, it starts all right, it starts going downhill fast. I'm falling apart! Getting old is *awful*."

I've heard a lot of statements like that and I bet you have too. The question is, do you believe them? Do you believe things automatically get worse as you age?

From birth, our bodies are changing—there's no denying that—but being stiff, having more aches and pains, feeling tired and "falling apart" are *not* normal aspects of aging. What we've done *with* and *to* our bodies—physically and mentally—is far more important than the number of years they've been around. It's what we've done—and haven't—up to this point that dictates the shape we're in right now.

I'd bet that was true for the woman on the phone, and it's certainly the case for ninety-three-year-old Tao Porchon-Lynch, only in a very different way. The world's current oldest living yoga instructor teaches classes six days a week, travels extensively and does competitive ballroom dancing on the international level with her twenty-three-year-old partner for fun. A few years ago, after she had hip replacement surgery, her doctor told her she would have to slow down. Tao sent him a picture proving him wrong. If you want to see just how wrong, look up the online photos of her in some amazing yoga poses. I am particularly in awe of the ones where she balances her body like a plank, holding herself up with only her hands—go ahead, give it a try yourself and let me know how it goes. Her motto is "Nothing is impossible." And it's true for her. What's true for you?

Now, if you're feeling rather uncomfortable about the state of your own body and abilities after reading that, don't make excuses. Suck it up and get tough with yourself. If you don't like the shape you're in or the level of activity you're currently capable of—get off your butt and do something about it. And if you catch yourself bemoaning your aches and pains or age like the woman in the store, stop it. Imagine that ninety-three-year-old dynamo staring you down, and turn whatever limitations, excuses or woes you just uttered into new empowering statements. Start saying things like *"It's great to be my age! I feel amazing! I can do anything!"* Vow to start living by *those* beliefs. Live your life as if you too know that *nothing is impossible.*

Trusting Yourself

Do you trust yourself? That's a loaded question, and for most of us, the answer is probably "Depends."

We might trust ourselves totally to do what we say when it comes to getting to work on time, but happily let ourselves off the hook for having a candy bar or not exercising, regardless of how many times we've sworn to do otherwise. We've all done that—we all *do that*—so the question is, why? There's really only one answer: We do what we really want to—even if it's for reasons we don't really understand.

We may know that munching on veggies is healthier than slurping on ice cream, but we want the ice cream anyway. It gives us what we want in the moment, even if we regret it later. And what we generally want in the moment isn't the ice cream, it's the pleasurable feeling that the ice cream will give us.

Same for not exercising. As you read in my story about flipping the mattress, I didn't want to exercise—even though I knew it would be good for me—because I had an inherent belief that I would feel worse afterward. I believed exercising would make me feel bad, so I found reasons not to do it. What was really going on, however, was that my subconscious mind was simply operating on its programming—exercise feels bad—and was keeping me from having to feel bad. It was giving me what I *really* wanted, regardless of what I said consciously.

So, what do you do about it? Recognizing where you're letting yourself off the hook and figuring out why is the most important step. Once I recognized the limiting belief, I flipped it around and rephrased it in my mind, then kept reminding myself of the new way of thinking. If I caught myself having the old thoughts, I stopped and repeated, "No, I always feel great when I exercise" or something similar. It kept me aware and it worked.

Now, what about the ice cream? Same thing applies, only in reverse. You have a belief that ice cream tastes good (and it does!) and that you will gain pleasure from it and will feel good. Well, that may be true in the moment, but it probably isn't true in the long run. Once the guilt kicks in and the effects of the sugar and fat start piling up, you'll feel bad, which means you'll need to find something to make you feel good—more ice cream. It's a vicious cycle.

So, if you're saying you shouldn't eat ice cream (or anything else), but you do anyway, then be honest and admit you like the stuff and are going to eat it. At least that way you aren't creating an internal conflict between what you say and what you do—and making yourself untrustworthy. But if you really wish your self-control didn't go out the window at the mere mention of pralines and cream or double chocolate fudge, then you have to change how you think and feel about the situation. And the way to do that—same as with the exercise—is to figure out what you really want for your life and what you're willing to do to get it. If what you really want is to be healthy, but you love being lazy and eating unhealthy foods, something's gotta give.

Since we can agree that you really do want to be healthy, the first thing you need to change is the way you feel about the things you do and the foods you eat. Sounds simple, doesn't it? Well, if you can just flip a switch in your brain and instantly make things different, good for you. I had to work for my changes. So, here are some things I did (we'll stick with the ice-cream example):

1. **Decided I could do whatever I wanted to:** First of all, I told myself that I could have ice cream whenever I wanted to—I'm an adult and it's my choice. I also had to agree that in so doing I was willingly choosing the consequences thereof.

2. **Owned my choice—no whining:** If I made the choice to eat ice cream, I couldn't say anything like "Oh, I really shouldn't." There would be no whining about how it made me feel fat or bloated later, and no yapping about how I wish I hadn't done it. If I chose to eat ice cream, I vowed to do it on purpose and with gusto.

3. **Linked ice cream with feeling bad:** I started really thinking about how I felt when I ate ice cream. Yes, it was tasty in the moment, but afterward I really didn't feel that great; I felt guilty and definitely wished I hadn't done it. So, I focused on that feeling—feeling really bad—while I thought about ice cream.

4. **Linked eating healthy with feeling good:** At the same time, I started noticing how great I felt when I ate fresh veggies and fruits and avoided high-calorie foods and fried things. I liked the way I felt inside my clothes and inside my mind, and I started really thinking about that while I looked over the choices on a restaurant menu, at a Chinese buffet or in my grocery cart.

It all began to snowball, and I very quickly developed strong positive associations with things that were healthy—I loved the way I felt and looked and I wanted to keep feeling and looking that way, or even better. I also naturally developed strong negative associations with things that weren't healthy. I didn't see yummy things anymore—I saw things that would make me feel bad. I wasn't ever depriving myself of anything or forcing myself to eat anything. I was simply taking the facts and making choices accordingly. In the process, not only did I learn that I could trust myself to do what I said, I also learned that I could trust my body to tell me what it wanted.

If the concept makes sense to you, give it a try. Combined with the new thinking about exercise mentioned earlier, you have two power-ful tools to help you make fast changes. Make a strong and conscious link in your mind between taking care of your body and feeling and looking good. Before you know it, you'll have developed a different relationship with food, exercise, health and fitness. There won't be any more angst over wanting what you can't have—you'll want what your body wants.

Remember, *you* are always the best authority on what is going on with *you*. Own that responsibility. Listen to your body and start trust-ing yourself to give yourself what you need. *You* are the authority in your life and you get to choose what you do—and why.

And remember those two "respectable option" questions from Chapter 3? You can use them here too:

- *Would someone with high self-esteem and self-respect do what I'm doing? Eat what I'm eating? Do the things I'm doing? Choose what I'm choosing?*

- *Will this get me closer to having the healthy body and good feelings I really want?*

It's all about choice. Make good ones!

TRANSFORMATION INSIGHT 17

List five things you do right now that you know are not healthy for you.
Describe how each is harmful and how you feel when you do it.

Unhealthy things you do	How it's harmful to you How you feel when you do it
1.	
2.	
3.	
4.	
5.	

List five things you do right now that you know are healthy for you. Describe how each is good for you and how you feel when you do it.

Healthy things you do	How it's good for you How you feel when you do it
1.	
2.	
3.	
4.	
5.	

List five new choices you can make, such as: get more sleep, eat different foods, exercise more or change particular beliefs. Explain why you want to make those choices and how they'll change your health, your mental outlook and your life. What will you be able to do then that you can't now?

New choice	Why you want to make the choice How it will change your life What you'll be able to do that you can't now
1.	
2.	
3.	
4.	
5.	

List five tips, techniques, insights or empowering beliefs that you want to remember to use.

1.

2.

3.

4.

5.

CHAPTER 18

IF ONLY...

*I lived on "if onlys" for a very long time,
and, like complaining, they made me feel like
I was doing something to fix my situation.*

Like most children, mine played the "if you loved me" game from time to time. I don't remember many specific incidents, although the "if you really loved me, you'd buy me a new BMW for my sixteenth birthday" was a memorable moment. Sometimes their antics worked and they got what they wanted. It didn't ever satisfy them for long, however. And that's the way with all of us. We think, *If only I could have that, then my life would be glorious and complete.* I certainly did it, even as an adult.

A favorite pastime of mine was making lists of things that I wanted my partner to do that he wasn't. If he would just start doing the things on my list, *then* I would be happy. Actually, all I was doing was detailing what I was willing to sell myself for. If he would just help out more around the house, call if he was going to be late, tell me before he vanished for days, promise not to flirt with other women, or tell me all the things I wanted to hear to make me feel good, then I could keep pretending that my intolerable situation wasn't.

I lived on "if onlys" for a very long time. Like complaining, they made me feel like I was actually doing something to fix my situation—but I wasn't. This next story isn't about me, although there are many parallels. I know what it feels like to be driven to do things even when you don't understand why—and even when they keep causing you pain.

I knew a young woman who had struggled for most of her life, trying to get other people to prove they loved her. The proof she required was for someone to "take care of her." If she could just find someone who would provide physical and financial support for her wants and needs—and allow her to do whatever she wanted whenever she wanted—then she would feel loved. It was a child's viewpoint, of course, and I would guess that she was trying—as we all do—to get what she hadn't had when she was growing up. She wanted so badly not to hurt anymore, and she believed that "if only" she could get someone to do all the things on her ever-changing list, it would prove that she was lovable, she would feel good about herself and her life would be magically transformed—and so would her unhappy past.

She used manipulation, blame, shame, guilt and wild demands—and, yes, "if you loved me, you would"—to try to force others to give her what she thought she wanted. No matter what anyone did for her, however, it flowed through her awareness like water through a sieve, draining the giver, but not filling her. Even when she got what she thought she wanted, she still felt empty inside and lost herself in one addiction or another.

In her mind, the blame for all her troubles fell squarely on the shoulders of others—parents, partner, boss, on and on. Nothing in her life was her fault—or her responsibility. She wanted people to feel sorry for her—it meant they cared. She used her sad story to get people to "help" in one way or another (money, food, attention), which made her feel taken care of and loved for a moment, maybe, but ultimately didn't give her what she really wanted. No one could ever do enough or give her enough to make her feel the way she wanted to.

In a way, her formula was correct. All someone *did* have to do was take care of her in the right way and then she *would* feel loved. In fact, that was exactly what she needed. However, there was only one person who could do that for her. The only person who could take care of her in the way she wanted and needed was the last person she was willing to demand it of—herself.

Tomorrow Is Up to You

As you know from the stories I've shared, like this young woman, I spent many years attached to being a victim. I based my choices on what I thought others needed or wanted, then blamed them when I wasn't happy. When I finally reached my limit on what I could take, it forced me to start looking at things differently. For me, starting to respect myself—and demanding that others respect me too—was a big step toward unraveling the underlying beliefs, fears, wounds and programming that were driving me. As I began to see things differently, I started making different choices—choices that honored me and made me feel good. I'm not perfect or bulletproof—not even close—but I *am* more aware of situations that could trigger old programming, and I do my best to make conscious choices about what I allow in my life.

Today, if my life isn't what I want it to be, I don't play the blame game. I know that the life I live is up to me. My parents, children, partner, boss, friends and pets are not responsible for the decisions I make or for the way I choose to live my life.

Your life is up to you too. You can choose to be a victim and blame everyone else for the way things are or use your "issues" as an excuse for why you didn't, couldn't, wouldn't or can't do something. You can play the "if only" game and let your past prevent you from taking responsibility for yourself today. You can do all those things if you want to—it's your life and your choice. However, I truly believe— no, *I know*—that if you've read this far in the book, you aren't doing that. You've already started making different choices—probably a lot of them. You've already made the leap from fearing the reflection in the mirror to saying, *"Show me more!"*

It probably hasn't been a cakewalk—it wasn't for me—and you may have found that not everyone is thrilled with the new you and your new approach to life. As uncomfortable as it may be at the moment, it's really a good thing! As you move forward, you give others the opportunity to move forward with you—some will, some won't. Either way, you ultimately win, because those who need to fall away will and you'll be free of their backward pull, which makes it easier to draw the people into your life who "get" the new you—who are as supporting and encouraging to you as you are to them.

Along the way, you'll have learned exactly what it really means to love and respect yourself. And the only wishing statements you'll be making are ones such as *"I love my life so much I just wish there more hours in the day to enjoy it!"* Sound like pie-in-the-sky? It isn't—*it's your future*.

So, let's get to it and ferret out some of those pesky "if only" wishes that are holding you back.

Turn Wishes into Actions

There are many kinds of "if only" statements we can make and not even realize it. They can be simple or complex, sometimes incorporating many "if this, then that" scenarios. Here are a few examples to get you thinking:

- If only I had a better boss, then I'd be happy.

- If only I had more money, then my wife would pay the bills on time and everything would be okay.

- If only my parents hadn't divorced, then I wouldn't have these problems.

- If only my husband didn't drink, then everything would be okay.

- If only my wife didn't shop and watch TV all the time, then the house would be clean and I wouldn't have to do everything myself.

• If my children would just behave, then my husband would stay home more and I wouldn't be so stressed.

Obviously, these statements aren't true. They are only exposing symptoms of much deeper issues. And let's get clear that these really are just wishes—they don't imply action of any kind. Take the first example. Someone who actually intended to *do* something about an unacceptable work situation might say, "I've tried everything I can to make things work at my job, but I am still not happy, so I am looking for a new one that is a better fit for me." That statement isn't a wish. It owns the problem and shows clear action toward dealing with it.

The last statement could become, "Because things are not okay in our family, the children are acting out and I am going to get to the bottom of it."

Let's take a simple example and play it out a little farther:

If only I had a new car, then I could do what I need to.

Okay, what do you need to do right now that you can't? How would you feel if you could do that right now? Do you have to get a brand-new car to make that happen? Why or why not? What will having a new car give you that you don't have right now? How will having a new car change your life?

It could be very simple—you need reliable transportation. You don't want to have to worry about the car you have breaking down and stranding you. Or maybe you want a vehicle that reflects your personality—who you are now, who you want to be or wish you were. You may be about to lose your job because you're always late due to car trouble. You may be ashamed to go anywhere because of how your car looks. Whatever it is, own it.

It is true that a flashy sports car won't make you cool or a better person anymore than driving a clunker makes you bad. *However,* your things, and how you take care of them, *are* reflections on what's going on in your life and your inner world. If you aren't taking care of yourself, you probably aren't taking care of your things either. Buying a new thing to replace the one you've neglected won't fix anything unless you fix yourself at the same time.

If you really do need or want a new car, wishing won't get you one—doing something will. When you get clear on *why* you want that new car—when you own your true feelings—then you'll automatically wire yourself to start doing things that will make it happen.

So, a more empowering statement would be: *"My car keeps breaking down and I'm getting a new one so that I can get to work on time and feel safe."* Now, *that* statement is going to make things happen!

Let's get to digging in your wishes pile and find some new statements that can get things happening for you too!

TRANSFORMATION INSIGHT 18

List three "if only" wishes (e.g., "If only I had a new car then I'd be able to do whatever I wanted").

1. If only _____

   then _____

2. If only _____

   then _____

3. If only _____

   then _____

Look at each statement carefully and decide if it's really true, then explain why or why not.

Is it really true?	Why or why not?
1. ☐ Yes ☐ No	
2. ☐ Yes ☐ No	
3. ☐ Yes ☐ No	

Using clues from your descriptions above, start digging into what you're really wanting out of the situation. For each "if only," describe how you'd *feel* if that wish came true (e.g., relieved, happy, safe, free, independent, worthy).

Then describe what conditions—physical and emotional—getting your wish would alleviate (e.g., worry about being stranded, feeling trapped, being late to work, losing job, depending on others, feeling like a loser).

How you'd feel if your "if only" wish came true	Physical and emotional conditions it would alleviate
1.	
2.	
3.	

Using the information from above, reword your wishes into empowering statements (e.g., Because my car keeps breaking down, I'm getting a new one so that I can get to work on time, keep my job and feel free, safe and successful).

1. _____

   _____

2. _____

   _____

3. _____

   _____

CHAPTER 19

MONEY, WORK AND LOVIN' IT

If you don't know what your beliefs are, you can't know the impact they have on your daily life or the choices you make.

I love my work! I love my money! Are those statements okay with you? Is it okay for you to love your work *and* love your money? You'll probably go along with me, at least consciously, about work—loving that is okay. But what about money? Loving *that* can set off all kinds of internal fireworks, so let's start there.

Love, Lust and the Root of All Evil

We know we have to have money—our world requires it—but most of our beliefs about money do not bring us loving feelings or joy. Start with the typical old sayings—it doesn't grow on trees, it's the root of evil and such. Most of us have heard those. However, we've heard things like these too: *Money is power. Time is money. A rising tide lifts all boats. A penny saved is a penny earned. Money makes the world go 'round*—or is that love?

It makes your head spin! And about that love thing. We already covered how many different meanings that word can have, so even saying that money isn't evil, it's the love of it that's evil, doesn't really help anything. In fact, I think it makes things worse. For me, the more appropriate word is lust—that makes sense to me. So, for clarity here, let's all agree that lusting after money is bad and allow love to carry the ball for nicer, more helpful thoughts. Follow along and I'll explain more why you don't have to be afraid to love money—why it isn't evil or any root thereof.

When I need to put a nail in a board, I am very grateful to have a hammer. One might even say that since that hammer makes life a lot easier for me, I love it—and I do! I love my car and my whirlpool bathtub for similar reasons. So, why not money?

Programming, plain and simple. We've all been imprinted with a mixed bag of messages about money, most of them shaming us for having it or wanting it. So, if you think about money right now, what do you feel in your body? Anxiety or joy? Nothing? Are you still busy trying to figure out what your beliefs are or filter them so they are "right" or good? Are you trying to line up your thinking with what you think it *should* be?

What Are You Thinking?

Do you know what you truly believe about money? Unless you've taken the time to look specifically at the issue, you don't. As we've already established, if you don't know what your beliefs are, you can't know the impact they have on your daily life or the choices you make.

We all have core beliefs about money, wealth, poverty, rich people, poor people, white collar, blue collar and everything in between, as well as the interactive nuances between them. We just generally don't realize we do. It's simply the way we are—it's our version of "normal" through our particular lens.

For example, if you grew up in a family where people were struggling for money and felt oppressed by their jobs, their bosses, company owners and others in positions of power, you probably have beliefs that reflect that. Some possibilities include: *"All rich people are greedy crooks. Rich people got their money by taking advantage of poor people.*

Rich people are selfish, mean and unhappy. I may not have much, but I work hard for my money and I'm proud I'm not like them. Look at them, showing off in their suits and fancy cars—they don't ever have to get their hands dirty. I'm smarter than they are, but they treat me like an idiot—they couldn't begin to do what I do. I do all the work and get nothing, and they do nothing and get all the credit and the money. I'll never get ahead, so there's no use trying. There's nothing I can do about it. It's just the way it is." Or a million other possibilities.

As I wrote those, it felt like a heavy dark cloud came over me, pushing me lower and lower, which is exactly what that sort of thinking does. It keeps you in a self-perpetuating downward spiral where the only thing you can do to "feel better" is complain more. You rant and rave about how horrible the situation is, how you are clearly being wronged and how there is absolutely nothing you can do about any of it. Venting your frustrations makes you feel better, because by God, you've given *somebody* a piece of your mind, even if it's only the bartender, your buddy or the family dog. Feeling vindicated, you pat yourself on the back for being able to put up with such incompetent and ignorant people—not many people could take what you do—then slip on your martyr's crown and keep doing exactly what you've been doing.

I bet you can think of someone right now who fits that description. You can probably see how the victim mentality and self-sabotage play into the scenario as well, and they all have their roots in unconscious limited thinking.

Let's take some of our common statements from above and find the underlying beliefs that might be fueling them.

Common Statements	Underlying Beliefs
1. All rich people are greedy crooks. Rich people got their money by taking advantage of poor people. Rich people are selfish, mean and unhappy.	People who have a lot of money are bad. Poor people are good. The only way to get a lot of money is by doing bad things. You can't be happy if you have money.
2. I may not have much, but I work hard for my money and I'm proud I'm not like them.	Work is hard. Life is a struggle. It's honorable to be poor and struggle. It's dishonorable to be rich and not have to struggle.

Common Statements	Underlying Beliefs
3. Look at them, showing off in their suits and fancy cars—they don't ever have to get their hands dirty.	Wearing nice clothes and having nice things is bad, a sign of a greedy, lazy person. The only honorable work is where you get your hands dirty.
4. I'm smarter than they are, but they treat me like an idiot—they couldn't begin to do what I do. I do all the work and get nothing, and they do nothing and get all the credit and the money. I'll never get ahead, so there's no use trying. There's nothing I can do about it. It's just the way it is.	People with power are ignorant and incompetent. No one will ever recognize my value. I am invisible. I am unworthy. Everyone is out to get me. Smart people are powerless. I am powerless.

From these simple examples, it's easy to see how someone who grew up around people making those kinds of statements—or who makes them himself—would have a difficult time feeling comfortable having money, being promoted or even enjoying his work. If your Belief Monkey is convinced that having money will make you a horrible person, it's going to do everything it can to keep that from happening. Your inner belief system is going to make sure you don't become stupid by being a boss either. And since struggling gives you honor, well, you're going to look for situations where you have to struggle. Makes total sense!

Just Enough

A few years ago, a friend of mine was in turmoil over money. She was working at a job that was physically and mentally difficult, and she was struggling financially. One day over lunch, as she had many times before, she voiced her desires to the universe. "I'm not asking for much," she said. "All I want is to have just enough to pay my bills with a little left over each month. Is that really too much to ask?"

She was in pain and her words were a desperate plea, as if begging God to explain why she was still struggling even after she'd lowered the bar as far as she could, all the way down to "just enough to get by."

"Well," I said, finally willing to tell her what she needed to hear and hoping she was ready to hear it. "If just enough is all you want, then that's all you'll ever have—just enough to get by. You'll be right where you are today, wishing for just enough and barely making it."

Yes, she was taken aback and a little angry—a lot of us are when we hear truth and don't like it—but I didn't back down. I asked her why it would be bad to have *more* than just enough. Who would suffer because she had fewer worries about money? Who would suffer because she had the freedom to buy things that she wanted and would enjoy? Who had to have less so she could have more? Why did she only deserve *just enough*?

She stuttered, stammered and started to defend and explain, then stopped as the lightbulb came on. The more we talked, the more my friend embraced the idea that it was okay to have more. As she realized it didn't make her noble or more spiritual because she was struggling financially—or bad or greedy if she wasn't—her face began to lighten and she began to sit up straighter. She also realized that if she wanted to help others, it would be a whole lot easier to do if she had money to do it.

By the time we finished our lunch, the words "just enough" were no longer in her vocabulary and she walked away feeling better than she had in months. Within two weeks, she had a new job, making *double* what she had been! Such is the power of beliefs.

More and Less

The reason I could say those things to my friend is because I have similar programming. One of the roadblocks that I've had to work with is the belief that there is only so much—if I have more, someone else must have less. It's just more scarcity thinking, of course, reinforced with guilt, shame and other social programming, such as "Don't take more than your share," "Don't be greedy" and "Don't be selfish."

While it's perfectly logical to stop a three-year-old from putting all the mashed potatoes on her own plate so there's enough for others, the subconscious takes those "don't take more than your share" messages and implements them literally and globally—forever.

People who have scarcity thinking will subconsciously and automati-

cally hold themselves back, stopping at whatever level the child's programming deems too much. They'll stop before they think they'll get in trouble
or be labeled bad. They also may feel guilty for wanting it in the first place
and will deny themselves the right to even considering having it. Yet, at
the same time, they'll resent those who do. They'll feel victimized by the
"haves," although they are the ones who've made themselves "have-nots."

Love Your Work

At the beginning of the chapter, you probably thought loving work
didn't have as much baggage attached to it as loving money did. The
limiting beliefs we've touched on about struggle and how it's honorable
to stay repressed might have changed your mind on that a bit. Of
course, you might also be wondering how many people actually do
love their jobs? How many people go to work because they *want to*
instead of because they *have to*?

We've all been admonished to do what we love and the money
will follow, but who really believes that? And doesn't it seem inherently wrong somehow to love your work? Besides, if you love what you
do then it isn't really work. You're getting paid to have fun—taking
money for having a good time. That can't be right, can it?

Those statements and questions make good sense—if you have the
limiting beliefs that support them. Did you catch the limitations and
recognize the underlying thinking that went with it? Can you see how
that kind of thinking once again backs you into a corner, demanding
that you work at a job you don't like?

Remember, your Belief Monkey only does what your subconscious programming tells him to. If he's operating off the beliefs that
you're not supposed to like your job, that honorable work must be
hard and that you have to struggle to get ahead, he's not going to let
you get into situations where you make a lot of money doing things
that are easy and fun for you.

For example, you might love playing the piano and have the innate
ability to hear a tune and play it instantly, but you'll dismiss it as noth-

ing because you—unlike most other people—don't have to work hard at it. Instead, you'd choose to dig ditches. You'd hate it, but since it's hard work, you'd feel like you were "earning" your money and would feel honorable. Make sense—or at least nonsense?

It's all about the beliefs. As long as you keep the same belief, you'll stay stuck having the same experiences that validate it. You *must* change your beliefs at the core level in order to change your experiences.

Turn Self-Limitation into Self-Transformation

The great thing about recognizing your limiting beliefs is that once you dig up all the details, you then have a recipe for reconfiguring them into statements that work for you instead of against you. Here are a few examples of some new empowering beliefs you could use to replace limiting ones. The first statement reworks our old "root of all evil" belief. Others turn the tables on lack, scarcity, making peace with money and loving work. Lots of ideas to spur thoughts about your own empowering statements.

- Money is the root of my financial health.

- I totally and completely release the need for struggle and allow myself to succeed with harmony, ease and joy.

- I respect, appreciate and utilize money effectively and joyfully in my life.

- The highest and most honorable calling is to follow my heart, because when I am living my highest potential and greatest joy, I am at my best for others.

- I am comfortable and at ease with having a lot of money.

- I love money! I love and appreciate how much freedom, relief and opportunity it provides me.

• I am grateful for the opportunities that being wealthy provides me on so many levels.

• Money is a tool like any other and I use it respectfully and effectively.

• I am so relieved and joyful at the freedom I feel now that I have plenty of money.

• It is okay for me to have more, just as it is for others.

• There is enough for everyone.

• It is such a relief to be free from struggle and stress and loving what I do. I love my work!

• The more money, love, joy I have, the more I have to share with others.

• I am so amazed at how great I feel now that I am following my heart, honoring my natural talents and abilities and living the life I love!

• I am so relieved that money is now abundant in my life.

• I love how much fun I am having now that money flows freely into my life.

• I love my job!

• I am so grateful that the work I do is also my passion and brings me purpose, fulfillment and prosperity.

• I love my life!

• I am so grateful to be earning such a fabulous six-figure income from doing what I love!

Wouldn't you rather have your Belief Monkey creating situations and experiences based on *those* kinds of beliefs?

Of course you would! And it's time to uncover the details you need to create your own specific belief statements. So, let's take a little trip back in time and see what might have created some of your specific limited thinking about money, work and wealth—and how to turn those thoughts into your very own new empowering beliefs.

TRANSFORMATION INSIGHT 19

Think about the economic and social background you grew up in. Without judging anything, let your mind travel back to conversations around the dinner table, or wherever family discussions typically occurred. Be the objective observer. See the scene and hear the words, but also look beyond and see what you could not as a child. Look at the situation with understanding for the time, the circumstances and the perspective of each person involved.

Use the following questions as a jumping-off point. Let any and all thoughts come up and be sure to write them down.

1. Looking back, do you feel that your parents or caretakers were happy? Why or why not? What specific words, circumstances or actions revealed their happiness or unhappiness?

2. How did they talk about their successes and accomplishments?

3. What kinds of problems did your family talk about? How did they talk about their frustrations, disappointments and challenges? What kinds of things did they say?

4. From what you know, the words they used and the things they did, what do you think they were afraid of?

5. For each person in your family—parent, grandparent, sibling or other significant relative—list what you think was his or her greatest disappointment.

6. What were their greatest successes? What were they most proud of?

7. What words or phrases did they use when talking about money, paying bills, buying things, work, jobs or lack thereof?

8. Did the people in your family feel respected? Why or why not?

9. How did they feel about people who had less?

10. How did they feel about people who had more?

11. What were your parents' most positive character traits related to work and money (e.g., hard working, generous, frugal)?

12. What character traits related to work and money caused them the most trouble (e.g., spendthrift, unreliable, gambler)?

Using the information from your answers above, make a list of at least five family beliefs (positive or negative) related to work, money, wealth, poverty, honor and success.

1.

2.

3.

4.

5.

Now that you have a clearer picture of your family's views, values and beliefs about money, work and success, look at your own. Following the examples below, list five limiting beliefs that you realize you have. Then reframe the limitation into a self-transformation statement that supports and empowers you.

Limiting belief	Empowering belief
Money is the root of all evil.	Money is the root of my financial health.
There's only so much to go around.	There is enough for everyone.
1.	
2.	
3.	
4.	
5.	

Create as many empowering statements as you can think of and start reading them daily. They'll also come in handy in later chapters.

CHAPTER 20

15 TOUGH-LOVE REMINDERS

When we take the courageous path and hold ourselves—
and each other—accountable, we open the door to joy.

We all want to be happy; that's a given. So why aren't we? The answer is generally pretty simple: What we *say we want* and what we *do* are two very different things. We say we want to be happy, but we make choices that bring us pain. We say we want our lives to be different, but we don't *do* anything different. We talk a good game, but we don't live it.

Below is a list that summarizes some of the self-improvement strategies in this book. Some may seem a bit harsh, but by this point, I hope you are able to be honest with yourself and see the value in simply "saying it like it is." When we take the courageous path and hold ourselves—and each other—accountable, we open the door to joy.

So, take a deep breath and dive in!

1. Grow Up

If you're still blaming anyone for how your life is, you're not living in the present and you have zero chance of being happy. Nobody had a perfect childhood—nobody—and a lot of people have lived through bad relationships, serious health issues and untold traumas. The reality is that whatever happened to you before now is located permanently in the past. Those chapters of your life are written and there are no rewrites. *No matter what you do, you cannot change what has already happened.*

You *can*, however, change how you feel about it and how you allow it to affect you—if you want to. If you don't, and you choose to hang on to your old story as your excuse for how awful your life is now, then do us all a favor and just admit it. Just say you like having people feel sorry for you. Admit that keeping your past alive gives you permission not to take responsibility for yourself and your life today. Of course, the only place that makes sense is in your head. Emotionally mature adults *demand* responsibility for their own lives.

2. Nobody Owes You Anything

Neither your mother, your father, your partner nor any government agency owes you a thing. It isn't your birthright to be handed everything on a silver platter. If you've had a free ride until now, don't think you're special, because it hasn't done you any favors. You haven't been cutely coddled, preciously pampered, indulgently spoiled or even enabled— you've been *disabled and retarded.* Sorry, but look up the definitions. If your parents made sure you never had to work and saved you from ever suffering any consequences, well, you *have* been held back and you *have* acquired a disability—and the last thing you need is to be rewarded for it.

The good news is that the condition isn't permanent. You can learn to take care of yourself and gain the self-respect and self-satisfaction that comes from it—if you want to. So, embrace it. Take responsibility for yourself and your life. You'll be amazed at how good it feels to accomplish things yourself—to be able to stand tall and say, "Yes, I did that!"

3. Suck It Up and Grow a Spine

Your life is a reflection of your choices. If you don't like what those choices have gotten you up to this point, suck it up and admit it, and then make different ones. Face the truth of what isn't working in your life and what you have to do about it—then do it. If you know your job is killing you, step back and figure out why. Assess the situation objectively, then either change your attitude or change your job.

If you're miserable in your relationship, you can bet your partner is too, so suck it up and address the situation honestly. Choosing to ignore reality and stay in pain is not only masochistic, it's insane, and if you had an ounce of self-respect, you wouldn't do it. So, grow a spine and make the choices that someone with self-respect would. And do not—even for one second—delude yourself that another person is going to change enough to make you happy. Whether it's at the office, at home, in the car or in outer space, your happiness is your responsibility, and the sooner you accept that fact, the sooner you'll start making choices that reflect happiness.

4. Take the "Kick Me" Sign off Your Back

If you feel like people take advantage of you all the time, you are not a victim, you are a volunteer. When you walk around with a chip on your shoulder and expect bad things to happen, you're just begging someone to do something to make you feel bad. Have yourself a big glass of self-respect, own your emotions and your reactions and deal with life head on. Getting your feelings hurt is for third grade. What everyone else is doing is not about you, so stop taking everything personally and start looking at situations objectively. Things happen, but you're only a victim if you decide to be.

5. Life Isn't Fair—Get Over It

You can spend your life bemoaning what's happened and how unfair it is, or you can put your attention on something productive and get on with living. Every minute you spend whining about how you were wronged is a minute of joy lost. You can't change the past—ever. And the more you stay focused on how unfair things are, the more unfair things you're going to find to feel sad and mad about. Learn from your past experiences, do your best to see that the same things don't happen again and get on with the business of having better, happier times—*now!*

6. Do Something About It or Shut Up

If you aren't willing to change your relationship or your job, then quit complaining about it and admit that you like being miserable. If you aren't willing to change your eating, drinking or exercising habits, then quit complaining about being fat, sick and tired. Either you want something different or you don't. If you do, then you have to *do* something different. Whatever you find yourself continually complaining about, either make changes or admit you don't want to and shut up about it.

7. Get Your Head Straight About Health

You can plan to be sick if you want to, but there is no law or genetic code that says you have to get a certain number of cold or flu episodes each year, so stop planning on it. Next year, if you "always" get three colds, then decide to get only two. Or just cut to the chase and change your belief to one that creates health, such as "I'm always healthy and never get sick." The sickly belief was working perfectly for you—you always got what you said you would—so there's no reason a healthy one won't work just as well.

Take a look at all your health issues and your health beliefs. Get brutally honest with yourself and see how your problems serve you, because in some way they do. Does being sick, overweight or otherwise unfit keep you from having to do things you don't want to? Does it make someone do what he or she wouldn't otherwise? Does it get you sympathy or paid time off from work? Does it give you something to focus on so you don't have to think about or deal with other problems in your life? Get to the bottom of why you have the beliefs about your health that you do. Then, if you're willing, change them to beliefs that serve you in a positive way. If you're not—if you want to keep your problems—be honest about it.

Health conditions that require medical attention really *do* require medical attention. If you need to see a doctor, see one. Just remember that there isn't any physical issue that can't be at least helped by a positive mental shift, so get your head straight and use it to help you stay well, not get sick.

8. Take Responsibility, Not Pills

If a situation is making you sick, don't go to the doctor for a pill to ease the symptoms so you can keep doing what's causing it—fix the real issue. Sure, you can take all kinds of things for acid reflux, depression, insomnia and a litany of other issues—you already know I did. Just remember, the real problem will not go away, and at some point, there will be a reckoning. Your pain is there for a reason, but if you don't heed the warning, what starts out as a stress response can turn into a serious condition that takes serious action. Don't let it get there—deal with the "inner" emotional issues first and you might be surprised how few "outer" physical issues you have that require extreme treatments.

9. What Are You Talking About?

If you're constantly complaining about things being a pain in the neck, you probably have some kind of issue in that area. If you're always saying that something or someone pisses you off, you can't really be surprised if you have problems with your bladder, kidneys and such. If you keep saying you're sick and tired of something, your body is probably agreeing with you. The words you say matter. So do your thoughts. Your stresses and worries *will* show up in your physical body in one way or another and your words are already telling you how, so pay attention. Change what you say to yourself—and deal with the real issue so your body doesn't have to.

10. Mosey Over to the Mirror

It's easy to point fingers and have great suggestions for how others can do better in their lives. When someone does something that *really* bothers you, you can probably come up with a quick list of character flaws, intelligence deficiencies and evil qualities as the reason. Fine and dandy, have a ball, but when you're done, mosey on over to the mirror with that list you just made and try it on for size. Whatever is bothering you about *them* is reflecting something about *you* that needs to be dealt with. It may be a direct reflection or it may be something that you've worked on, moved past or just don't want to be around anymore. Whatever the case, it's about *you*. Get down to the whys of your feelings and things will make a lot more sense.

11. Stop Waiting for Someone Else

You can sit and wait, and wish and hope, that something or someone will change, miraculously transforming your life in the process. Or you can get up off your butt, take responsibility for your own life and start transforming it yourself. And stop all the "if only" nonsense. *"If only he'd buy me flowers, then I'd know he cared, then it would be okay."* No, it wouldn't, and a lack of foliage isn't your problem—*you* are your problem. You aren't unhappy now because you aren't getting gifts. You are unhappy because you're in a situation that isn't working and you're looking for ways to pretend it is. Stop it. Whatever is on your mental list of things he can do to fix the situation—won't. You cannot make someone do enough—or change enough—to make you happy. You are the only one who can fix things for you. Get to it!

12. If You Want Different, Do Different

It's very simple. If you want a chocolate cake, you can't use the lemon cake mix you always buy. If you want something different from what you have right now, then you have to do something different from what you're doing. If you want others to treat you differently, start treating yourself differently. If you want others to act differently, start giving them a good example to follow. Stop complaining and start being the person you think everyone else ought to be. Take responsibility for the way things are in your life. If you want different outcomes, make different choices.

13. If You Don't Know, You Can't Get

If you can't define what you want—or *why* you want it—the odds of you getting it are just about zero. And some flip, offhand answer like *"Oh, I know what I want"* doesn't cut it. If you haven't taken the time to think about what your dream life looks and feels like—what it would be like to live it—then you don't know. You do not have tangible, achievable goals—you have airy-fairy "someday" wishes.

Take the time to sit down and map out your dream life—yes, there's a template in this book. Get in the habit of asking yourself why you want what you want. By understanding the real reasons behind your desires—which are the feelings you get from them—you can make conscious choices that create what you want effectively.

14. Train Your Belief Monkey

Defining the dream is essential, but it's also essential to know what's lurking in the shadows to keep you from having it: your limiting subconscious beliefs. Doing your work, defining your dream and visualizing it every day are great, but they aren't enough—not even close. Besides actually doing the work to make it happen, you also have to make sure your internal voice—your unconscious or subconscious mind—is on the same page with your conscious one.

Just because you say you want a big house with a pool and an outdoor kitchen doesn't mean your inner Belief Monkey is going to go along with you. If your hidden programming tells you that people who live in big houses with pools are bad, greedy, selfish and mean, you won't be getting the big house anytime soon. What you believe about yourself and your worthiness or ability to have what you want is critical. So, get down to the deepest level, find your limited thinking, reword those beliefs into ones that support your goals and retrain your monkey to work with the good stuff. Then, before you know it, you'll be buying new furniture to fill up the new house and firing up the grill for a pool party. Change your beliefs and you change your world.

15. Do It on Purpose

The great thing about knowing what you want is that it makes it very easy to do things on purpose. When you're actively in charge of your life, you aren't just drifting along, letting things happen, reacting and fighting fires as they come up—what you do has purpose. When you have a clear goal, you know what will get you closer to it and what won't, and you don't get caught up in distracting dramas or other nonsense. And if you do get triggered, you immediately look for the why and deal with it. When you're living on purpose, you don't have time to waste on things that hold you back. So, whatever you decide to do, do it deliberately and on purpose.

TRANSFORMATION INSIGHT 20

List the three topics, comments, strategies or suggestions from this chapter that irritated you the most and explain why.

Topic	Why it irritated you
1.	
2.	
3.	

Now list the three topics, comments, strategies or suggestions that inspired or motivated you and explain why.

Topic	Why it motivated or inspired you
1.	
2.	
3.	

CHAPTER 21

SO, WHAT DO YOU WANT?

*I'm not sure what scared me most, that I didn't
know what I really wanted—or that I did.*

Now that you've faced the mirror, pushed through the reality muck
and learned to play nice with your Belief Monkey, you've probably
noticed things changing in your life. The fears and limiting beliefs
that had been calling the shots may not be doing so as much anymore,
because you've learned to call them out and make the process work
for you.

You've also probably become very clear about respecting yourself—and demanding that others do too. You've started setting healthy
boundaries and taking care of yourself better than you ever have before.
With all those great accomplishments under your belt, it's time to get
down to the very heart of the matter. It's time to start pulling everything together and get to the point of why you picked up this book in
the first place—to start living the life you love. So let's get started with
that one defining question: What do you want?

Yes, it sounds very simple, but it isn't. As we touched on a bit
in the last chapter, you have to know what you want in order to get
it. You have to define your dreams in order to make them realities.
However, a lot of us get tripped up by the question itself. The idea
of putting words to our most secret desires can feel both trivial and

profound, simplistic and overwhelming, silly and absolutely terrifying. More than once, when confronted with that question, I froze like the proverbial deer in the headlights. I'm not sure what scared me most, that I didn't know what I really wanted—or that I did.

It took a long time for me to own up to my own truth, but lucky for you, you've already done the hard part and are ready to dream big, dream clear and dream for real. It's time to put all that soul searching to work for you and get down to the nitty-gritty of defining what you want your life to be.

Start with whatever comes to mind first: a new car, a new job, a relationship, a home, a business, a feeling, anything. No matter what you choose to work with, you'll find important insights into what makes you tick. And once you go through the process with one thing, it's a snap to go through it with another.

One thing you don't want to do, however, is paint specific people into your picture unless you're dreaming the dream together. Whether it's a spouse, significant other, business partner or someone you wish might be in your life, if you aren't actively sharing a vision with them, don't do it. And, as a side note, if you can't talk honestly about your desires with that person, you aren't at a place to live the dream together anyway. So, if that's the case, focus on the type of person, traits and characteristics you want, how you'd feel about and with him, and allow the right person to show up.

Now, if you and your mate are planning to travel the world together, live in the Bahamas on a yacht or buy a mountain chalet—if you're actively envisioning the same picture together—then absolutely include that! It's also okay to envision having happy interactions with others—see yourself getting along with your kids, parents, friends, coworkers and such. Just don't create a dream life for someone else—it won't work.

In my own case, I had a vision of what I wanted in my relationship, where I wanted to live, the type of house we'd live in, what we'd be doing and so forth. The problem was that I was also only willing to see one particular person in the picture with me, and it was a picture he had no idea about. I painted my partner into a dream he didn't share and it was a disaster.

While you don't want to include someone in your dream who isn't dreaming it with you, you do have to be specific enough. You can't just say, "I want a relationship." Unless you've defined what that means, you're saying you're open to having *any* kind of relationship— anything from dating someone who's also dating ten other women to being married to someone you aren't in love with. But that's not really true, is it? So, get your vision of what you want—the specifics and the feelings—clear in your head.

Since relationships are pretty important to most of us, here are some questions that can help define the kind of situation and person you're really looking for. Resist the temptation to find ways to make a certain person fit your true desires—or to adjust your desires to fit the person. This is about you and getting clear about what kind of person you want to be with and what experiences and feelings you want from the relationship. So, if you're looking for a mate, honestly answering the following questions will give you some amazing insights on what you're really looking for.

- What kind of relationship do you want—casual dating, committed significant other, marriage or other arrangement?

- What kind of person is your perfect partner?

- What does he value? What's important to him?

- What does he do that you admire?

- How does he treat you?

- How do you feel when you're with him?

- Why is it important for you to be with a man like him?

- When you see yourself with him, what are you doing? Are you having fun? Exploring? Learning things?

- How do you act when you're with him? Relaxed and peaceful? Laughing hysterically? Just being yourself?

- What do you like about *you* when you're with this man?

Answering these kinds of questions helps you define your dreams in real-world terms. It may turn out that the very person you wanted in your picture will be. But until you're really clear on what you want—what living your dream life with your dream partner looks and feels like—you can't get it . . . with anyone.

Go through this same kind of process with as many aspects of your dream life as possible—work, career, business, home, stuff and other goals. Be sure to keep good notes, because the information will be helpful when you're defining your dreams and making them come alive. The more details and feelings you've identified, the easier it will be to see and feel your new life as if you're already living it.

And, along with using your new reframed beliefs, you are systematically overriding your fears and limited thinking—you're retraining your Belief Monkey to work *for* you. Now, instead of doing whatever was necessary to keep you away from your dream because he believed you didn't deserve it, he'll be on the lookout for situations and circumstances that will get you closer to it.

When you become comfortable with your desires—when they already seem real—you'll automatically start doing things to move you toward them. And when you can see it and feel it and are taking actions toward it, then you'll have it. Here's another little equation to sum up where we're headed with all this:

See + Feel + Do = Have

Imagining and envisioning are just wishful thinking without the doing and there won't be any having. So, it's time to pull it all together, define your dreams and figure out what to do about them. Gather up all your wishes, wants, dreams and desires—big and small—and get ready to run them through . . .

The Dream Distiller

This chapter's Transformation Insight *is* the Dream Distiller. It's a list of specific questions that get you focused on your goal, help you understand why you want it, help you see it and feel it as if you already have it, and define how you're going to start taking action to get it.

The Dream Distiller can be used for absolutely anything. It works for defining the big picture of what you want your life to look like as well as for "stuff" goals. A house, marriage, car, boat, world travel, awards, a college degree, a child, your name in lights on Broadway and a new career are just a few possibilities. Make copies of the template and use them again and again. Not only does it get easier to work the process, you also wipe out more limiting beliefs and expand your thinking, your life and your joy.

The Dream Distiller starts with a group of questions I like to call The Big Four, because they're little questions that pack a big punch. They seem simple and seemingly straightforward, and you may be tempted to just gloss over them, thinking that they're silly and that you know the answers. Well, they aren't silly, and unless you've taken the time to think about these things in depth, you really don't know the answers.

The Big Four

1. What do you want?

2. Why do you want it?

3. How will it make you feel if you get it?

4. How will you feel if you don't?

Memorize these. Then, when you're making a decision or choosing one thing over another, you can run the options through this filter. You'll get a deeper understanding and clarity about what you're really wanting from it, which can help you make wiser decisions. You can use these questions for just about anything—even buying a new pair of high heels or a fishing lure.

Yes, it may sound tedious when you very well know you need a new pair of red shoes to go with the new dress, or that the fish are biting on purple worms with spinners, but do it anyway. You might find out some things about yourself that will surprise you. Using the questions will help define the real underlying *why*—particularly the feeling you're really looking for—so you can decide if what you're considering is the best way to get it. The questions are also good for uncovering limiting beliefs.

In the following example of Big Four answers, a man is very unhappy with his job and wants to quit. As you read through, notice his perspective on the situation and the words he uses as he talks about it.

Example 1:

1. **What do you want?** Quit my job.

2. **Why do you want to quit your job?** I hate it and I want out. It's long hours and low pay, and I'm barely making ends meet. That's bad enough, but my boss treats me like a child—like I don't have a brain in my head. Nobody's happy there, and with all the bickering and backbiting, well, it feels like I'm back in high school. I hate it.

3. **How will it make you feel if you quit?** Relieved, vindicated, free. I'd show them that I didn't have to take it anymore, that I was better than that.

4. **How will you feel if you don't?** Trapped. Victimized. Sad, depressed, worthless, and like I'm as dumb as they think I am. I'll feel like there's no hope of things ever getting better for me and that I'll never get ahead. It makes me sick to think that I'll be doing this for the rest of my life and working there until I die.

Being honest about your thoughts and feelings is essential. In this example, the deep feelings of unhappiness are a big motivator for change—for getting out of the situation. In coaching terms, that is a "moving away from" goal. The strong negative feelings may get you *out* of a bad situation, but they won't automatically get you *into* a good one. It's courageous and empowering to choose to leave a situation that isn't working for you. Having a positive goal to move *toward*, such as a new job you love, is even more empowering.

Let's try The Big Four questions again from a very different perspective. Notice how the outlook and attitude in this scenario create much brighter options out of the same unhappy situation. This time we'll keep going with the rest of the Dream Distiller questions and sample answers so you can see how things start to come together when you're moving toward your dreams.

Example 2:

1. **What do you want?** I want to quit my job and start my own window-washing business.

2. **Why do you want to start a window-washing business?** I really love washing windows. I don't know why, I just do. It's fun for me. I want to be my own boss, call my own shots and set my own hours. I like managing things and I'm good at it. I also like that in my new business, I can be somewhere different every day, meeting new people.

3. **How will it make you feel if you do?** Excited! Relieved! Free! In charge of my own destiny. I'll feel like I finally have some control over my life and that I'm living up to my potential. I'll be having fun too! Yes, I know it will be hard work, but that's part of it and I'm looking forward to it. I'll feel a bit scared too, though. This is a big step for me, but I've been running things where I am now, so I know I can do it. I'm nervous, but it's a

good nervous. I know it's up to me and I'm ready to go. Having my own business will make me feel proud, worthwhile, happy, fulfilled, and I'll also like myself. I'll feel like I've accomplished something, that I have a purpose. I can't wait!

4. How will you feel if you don't? Well, I'm *going* to do it, so there is no "don't" or "can't" in my vocabulary anymore. It is just a matter of timing. But, if I believed I couldn't have my own business and had to keep doing what I hate, well, I just can't think about it—I won't think about it, because I *am* starting my business. If it's not as successful as I want to be right away, I'll be a little disappointed, but I won't give up. I'll feel good no matter what, because I went for my dream and nobody can take that away from me.

The next step after you answer The Big Four questions is to make your goal come alive—to think about what your life would look and feel like if you already had it, were already living it, right now. You've probably been encouraged to do this before, but have you ever really done it? Have you been so immersed in your imagination that you laughed, cried or got goose bumps? If you think achieving your goal will bring you relief or peace, could you make yourself feel it? Feeling it—really feeling it—is what kicks your subconscious mind into action. So, let's start stirring up the images and feelings around your selected goal or your dream life.

What does your world look like now that you have your dream? Where are you? What things do you see around you? What kinds of people are with you? What sounds do you hear? A cheering crowd? A cash register ringing up sales? Gentle waves lapping on a beach? How does it smell? Is there food cooking in the kitchen? Do you smell fresh-cut grass? Hot dogs and mustard from the street vendor? Fragrant flowers? Is it warm or hot? Cold or balmy? Are you curled up in front of a fireplace or lounging on a boat in the sun?

Okay, you get the idea on visualizing your dreams, so now let's take the next step and take action in the real world to start turning them into reality. Personally, I was always a big fan of the *I Dream of Jeannie* and *Bewitched* methods, but the blinking and nose twitching never worked for me, so, I guess we'd better figure it out for ourselves. You've already worked with these next questions in different ways throughout the book, so they'll sound familiar—you know what to do with them.

Let's see what our window-washer friend is thinking about his dreams and what he's going to do about them.

1. **What will your life look and feel like when you have your window-washing business?** I am on the outside of an office building, the sun is shining and I'm looking at the reflection of the ocean in the glass. I'm wearing shorts and a T-shirt and I'm smiling and singing along with the music on the radio, matching my strokes on the glass to the rhythm. A light breeze is blowing across my face and I can smell the fresh, salty air. Every now and then, I get a whiff of the frangipani blooms on the trees around the building. I can't keep from smiling! I love my work! I love my life!

2. **What are you willing to do to have your business?** I'm willing to sell my house and invest the capital in equipment and startup costs. I'll learn every aspect of the business, but use pros to help me with accounting and taxes because I want that set up right from the beginning. I know I'll be working day and night at first to get things going, and I'm good with that, excited about it even. My social life can wait, and my friends will understand and maybe even help me out on some things.

3. **What are you not willing to do?** I'm not willing to compromise my ethics or anyone's safety. I'm not willing to envision an unrealistic fantasy scenario or pretend there aren't problems if there are. I won't take advantage of anyone or lie about things to get by.

4. **What could keep you from getting what you want?** Money. Fear. My house might not sell, or I might not get the amount of money for it that I need. I might not be able to buy equipment or hire employees.

5. **What can you do to overcome those obstacles?** I can make sure my house is in the best shape possible for showing and do some advertising myself to find buyers, so I have the best chance to get a good sale price. I can take a part-time job or sell some things. I can scale back one employee and the associated equipment. I think I could make that work for a short time until I build up enough jobs to hire the extra person. I can explore options for a small business loan or a personal loan.

6. **What is one thing you can do as a positive step toward your goal today?** I can work on the website for my business so that it will be ready to go when I get the funding. I can also do more research and add to my list of potential clients. I can get online and register my company name, get a business license and set up my sales tax account. I can call and check on the cost of ads. I can make flyers, write letters to send to potential clients and design my business cards. I can do a lot of things right now!

Do you see how one thing leads to another? The more effort you put into thinking about a goal as a reality, the more ideas pop up to make it one. Let every thought come up and acknowledge every feeling, even if you don't like them. Get everything out on the table—including your Belief Monkey—so that if you uncover any fears or limiting beliefs, you can immediately reframe them and get every level of your consciousness working for you.

This is where you pull it all together, define your dreams and get moving toward them, so don't hold back on anything. We started this book with getting clear on what you were willing to do and what you weren't. If you have others in your life to consider, the aspects of how your decisions affect them must be addressed realistically. Now is the time to do that.

For example, if you want to take a dream job in Alaska, but your wife's career doesn't allow for that or your son has one year left in high school, you have to address how you're realistically going to deal with those situations. This process isn't about creating pie-in-the-sky fantasies, it's about defining your heart's desires and turning them into reality in the most appropriate way for you.

Okay, now it's your turn to start defining, distilling, developing and *doing* your dreams!

TRANSFORMATION INSIGHT 21

The Dream Distiller

1. What do you want?

2. Why do you want it?

3. How will it make you feel if you get it?

4. How will you feel if you don't?

5. Make it real: What does your world look like now that you have your dream? Where are you? What do you see around you? What kinds of people are with you? How does it sound? Smell? What's the climate? What are you spending most of your time doing and where?

6. What are you willing to do to have what you want? What actions are you willing to take to make your dreams reality? What will you do in order to live the life you love?

7. What are you not willing to do? What are your parameters? What lines will you not cross? What limitations do you need to work within?

8. What could keep you from getting what you want? Play the "worst-case scenario" game.

9. What can you do to overcome that obstacle? For every possible problem you found, find at least two ways to get around it or keep it from becoming a roadblock.

10. What is one step you can take toward your goal right now?

11. How will it feel to get that step completed and be on your way to your dreams?

12. List other things—even small ones—you can do to move forward toward your dream.

Additional notes:

Copy this form and use it as a template for each of your goals, from the very specific material things to the global, life-changing ones. The more you do, the more you know, and the quicker you'll make things happen.

CHAPTER 22

THE VISION BOARD

*If I'd waited for others to agree that what
I wanted was possible, or that I was worthy
of having it, I'd still be waiting.*

Now that you've defined your dream goal, how about a few shortcuts to achieving it?

There are two techniques that I have found to be very powerful and, as the title of this chapter says, one is creating a vision board. The other is creating a vision sript, which is explained in detail in Chapter 23.

You may have heard a vision board called by a different name—dream board, dream map, treasure map or the like. Whatever you call it, a vision board is a collection of photos, symbols and other visual items that represent the things, situations and feelings you want to have in your life. Vision boards often also include inspirational and motivational quotes, key words or phrases that encourage or evoke particular feelings—anything that builds positive emotion around the dream and reinforces it as reality for you as you look at it. It turns hazy "someday" wishes into clear specifics that define what you're ready to start living now—and gives you a jumpstart to actually doing it.

By creating an image of what you want and making yourself feel as if you already have it, you're setting up a cognitive dissonance. Sounds like a bad thing, doesn't it? Well, it really means you've created a mental conflict for yourself. And, yes, you'll probably feel a bit off balance at first, because what you're telling yourself is real and what you're actually living don't match. That's the point. In order for you to have mental peace, what you envision and what you experience in reality *must* align. If you aren't living the life you want, one of two things has to happen. Either your mind has to decide it wants your current reality, or your current reality has to change to match what your mind wants. Pretty simple. Either way, you have to do something—you either back off on your dreams or start taking action to make them reality.

Since I know you're going all in on making your dreams come true, let's get to the nuts and bolts.

Vision Board 101

You can make your vision board out of poster board, cardboard, the back of a large notepad or even a sheet of paper. You can cut out photos that inspire you from newspapers or magazines and add your own phrases and other personalized touches. It can be one page or many. You can have one vision board for a single dream or combine many dreams on one page. It's your new life and you can create it and arrange it in any way you want to.

If you have a particular kind of house you want, or a specific setting or area you want to live in, put pictures of that on your board. If you want a great relationship, find photos that represent the *feeling* you want from it. Whatever it is—a new car, travel, school, a degree or certification, an organic garden, skydiving or being debt-free—use images that represent your dreams and inspire you to go for them. Always be sure to include your own face in your dream life in as many ways as possible.

I prefer to use my computer to design my vision boards because it's easy for me and I can quickly modify it whenever I want to. For those of you who are graphics pros, you can use your skills and software to put yourself authentically in all kinds of situations. Do it! Since that's not my thing, I use Microsoft Word and simply insert photos and text boxes into a document file.

The sample at right was created that way and uses some of our window-washer friend's goals from the earlier example. The top left image represents his successful business and the other photos fill out the rest of his dream life—where he might want to live and travel, what he wants to do and have, including a new relationship. There's a larger version of this example in the Transformation Insight below so you can see the details. However, since I didn't have a real face to put on our friend, I didn't insert him into any of the photos as you'll do with your own images.

Actually, that's the part that's the most fun for me, because when I put myself into a dream scene as if I'd been there when the photo was taken, I really do feel it. It feels exciting and real, and I can't help but say something like, *"Oh, yeah, this is for me!"* My current dream-house photo has me in a formal dress by the front door as if welcoming guests. Even with limited design options, it looks very real and I love it! It's also one of my screen saver images. The one of me in a swimsuit on a beach I've never been to is another favorite, as is the one with me in a jaunty pose beside "my" pool. Seeing myself already "there" in those photos triggers strong feelings for me and makes it easy to imagine living that life.

Another thing that I find powerful is taking an image of my bank statement and changing the amount to a new inspiring figure. At first, it can seem like a lofty fantasy, but after looking at it for a while, it doesn't seem ridiculous at all. There are no more "yeah, that'll never happen" feelings. It's just a number and I'm comfortable with it—and comfortable seeing it on my bank statement.

For Your Eyes Only

Don't hold back on dreaming or creating your dreams on your vision board. Make it as real and fabulous as possible. And after you've finished your masterpiece, you'll need to find a great spot to put it for viewing. If you've created a paper version—cut-and-paste or a printed copy from an electronic file—you'll want to put it in a place where you can see it but others can't.

Your dreams and your vision board are just for you—no one else. These are your dreams and you don't need to hear anyone else's opinions—or sense their silent judgments—about them. Even those you think would be supportive might not be. Your dreams could make *them* uncomfortable, and although it might not be intentional, they could start discouraging you for their own reasons, because of their own fears. As I said earlier, if I'd waited for others to agree that what I wanted was possible, or that I was worthy of having it, I'd still be waiting. So, don't go there. Keep this to yourself, and don't let *anyone* put *their* limitations on *your* dreams.

While it is for your eyes only, you still need to put your vision board in a place that's part of your normal routine where you'll be sure to see it—and use it. If you live alone, you could hang a printed version on your bathroom mirror or on your refrigerator—you could even put it *in* the refrigerator. The back of a closet door will work. So will your underwear drawer. Put your vision board in places where you'll see it frequently, because seeing it reminds you to stop and take a few moments to live it. Before long, those not-yet-real situations will feel as normal and familiar as the face in the mirror.

Because no one else uses or sees my computer, I use my vision boards and images from them as screen savers and desktop backgrounds. Whenever an image pops up, I live it for a few moments, seeing and feeling it. I read the personalized details of what occurs when that life is a reality. It can be anything—airline flight schedules or trip itineraries, summaries of financial details, book covers, quotes from great reviews, whatever I'm projecting into my life at that moment.

This stuff works, so set a regular time to sit with your vision board and imagine yourself in those scenes, having that lifestyle and that stuff, and feeling the way you'll feel when you do. First thing in the morning and just before you go to sleep at night are optimal times. The process doesn't need to take long, just a few minutes of living your dream.

The more you work with it, the more familiar the images will become—the more they'll seem like they're just a regular part of your life. Before long, it will seem perfectly normal for you to be standing beside your new sports car, walking hand in hand with your soul mate or looking out across the vistas of an exotic locale. Your mind will simply be thinking, "Of course, that's my life!" And your Belief Monkey will be busy looking for ways to create it.

Now that you know all the ins and outs of vision boards, it's time to build your own!

TRANSFORMATION INSIGHT 22

Create your own vision board based on the information you developed using your Dream Distiller. Place your vision board in places where you'll see it—but others won't. Look at it each day and imagine yourself in it. See it, feel it and enjoy it! Here's a general example based on our window-washer friend's dreams to inspire you. Be creative!

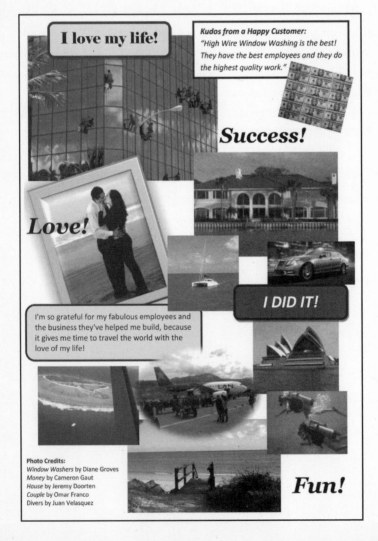

CHAPTER 23

THE VISION SCRIPT

*Your vision script gives you a written and
an auditory link to your subconscious—it's the
ultimate Belief Monkey retraining tool.*

Now that you've figured out what your dream looks like on your vision
board, it's time to figure out what you're going to tell yourself about it.
What words and phrases can you use to remind yourself how great it
feels and how glad you are to be living this fabulous new life?

Your vision board gives you a visual tool to help you generate the
feelings of already living the life of your dreams. Your vision script
gives you a written and an auditory link to your subconscious—it's
the ultimate Belief Monkey retraining tool. And, as we know, once the
little guy is on board with a new belief—once it becomes real on the
inside—it's going to become real on the outside.

A vision script is a series of positive, affirming and emotive statements that intricately define the specific things and feelings that you
want in your dream life. Basically, it's the words you would use to
describe what you're seeing and feeling when you look at your vision
board—what you might say or feel if you were really living it. It's a
written script for your life that you read every day. You can also record
it and listen to it with headphones, which is what I prefer.

There's a detailed sample script in the Transformation Insight below that you can use to develop your own personalized version, so don't worry about having to come up with everything on your own. It's already there, ready for you to modify, so let's just get a better feel for the kinds of statements you'll want to use to describe your own specific goals. Here are a few Do's and Don'ts to keep in mind.

Do's and Don'ts

Do use present tense for vision script statements, wording them as if they've already occurred. Some examples: *"I love my new home! It's so exciting to travel to different countries and I love all the new things I'm learning. I'm so glad I learned to speak the languages. I use my new skills everywhere I go and it makes things so much easier—and fun!"*

Don't use negative words to make positive statements. Saying *"I'm glad I'm not afraid to ride on elevators anymore"* won't help. As you probably know, you need to avoid using words such as *not, never, no* and so on, so that your subconscious mind gets the right message. You might be sick of living in the heat and humidity, and might even think and say such things as *"I am so sick of living in this sticky heat and never want to live where it's hot and humid again!"* Those kinds of statements can have a lot of passion in them, but your statements and affirmations need to focus on what you do want rather than what you don't. So, instead, say, *"I'm so relieved I'm finally living where it's cool and the air is crisp. I love playing in the snow, and I feel more energized, motivated and happy than I ever have."* See the difference?

Don't use conditional phrases, such as "I'll be happy *when*" or "I would be happy *if,*" because they imply that you aren't happy now and put distance between you and what you want. "I'm so happy to have . . ." or "I'm so happy now that . . ." are better options.

Do use your own idiosyncrasies and catch phrases in your statements to make them as real as possible. If you often say, "That blows me away" or "It was a snap," then use that in your script. If you say hot, cool, awesome, fantastic or whatever, use those words because they have built-in meanings and emotions for you that will amp up the power of your script even more.

Let's go through a few more examples, starting with wanting a new car. The following statement isn't a good one for a vision script: *"I'll be glad when I can get rid of this piece of junk and get a new one so I won't be worried about it breaking down and stranding me."* Knowing what you don't want—an unreliable car that leaves you stranded—is important, and it can be motivating. However, for a vision script, you only focus on what it will feel like *after* you're on the other side of the situation. Your statements reflect what you'll feel like after the piece of junk is history, when you have reliable transportation and are free of worry, such as *"What a relief it is to have a car I can depend on. It's so easy to just hop in and go whenever I want to. I love it! I feel so free!"*

Here's another statement that's positive and in the present tense, but just doesn't go anywhere. *"I live in a new house on the beach."* It technically fits the criteria, but it doesn't really make you feel anything. Think of how much more powerful it would be if you said the following instead:

> *I love living in my new, luxurious five-bedroom Mediterranean-style home on the gorgeous white-sand beach in Florida. My house is absolutely fabulous, and living here is even more wonderful than I imagined. I love all the tropical flowers around the house; they're all so beautiful and I love how there's always something blooming and some sweet fragrance around to smell, especially the honeysuckle and jasmine—they make me feel at home. I love looking out at the beautiful blue ocean from my office windows, and I love that I can walk down to the beach any time I want to and feel the warm sand beneath my feet. I feel so free, joyful and alive! I'm so happy; I'm smiling all the time! I am happier than I have ever been in my life!*

Now, *those* statements come alive—you can feel them. They're specific and detailed, and they have emotion. There's no question about what fulfilling that dream would feel like. Those are the kinds of statements that will get you moving.

Reality Resistance

When you first start writing down specifics, such as wanting to earn a particular amount of money or have something that seems ludicrous in your current situation, your mind may rebel. Thoughts such as "You've never had anything remotely close to that and you never will" may pop up. When you notice one of those thoughts, you know it's your Belief Monkey at work, so you know you need to give it a new mission. Reword your self-limiting belief into a self-transforming one that will work for you, such as *"This has always been for me, and now it's time! I deserve to have this and I accept it now! It feels so good to finally be able to relax and enjoy my life!"* Use your own specifics, of course. Emphasize the feelings you'll have when your dream is reality. Relief is one that I use a lot because my mind is comfortable with relief—I'll allow myself that. Use what works for you, then add your new statements to your vision script.

If you get a really strong negative reaction to a goal—the Belief Monkey just won't buy into it—you may need to take things in stages to make it easier for your mind to accept. If you put things out of the realm of believability for yourself, your mind will just ignore it. For example, if the most money you've ever earned in a year is $25,000, vowing to make $750,000 the next year might be a bit much. It's happened—it's more than possible—but it may not be something you want to tackle all in one bite.

There's nothing wrong with setting smaller goals that you can wrap your mind around and achieve more quickly. When you meet one goal, you'll have more confidence with the process and can raise the bar to your new comfort level and set another goal. The idea is to set believable and achievable goals that you can start bringing alive right now.

Get in the Right Mood

If you record your script—and I strongly recommend you do—you'll probably find yourself naturally putting emotion into your voice, because you really will be feeling it—it *will* seem real and you'll get excited. That's the idea! Don't be afraid to ad lib either. If you're feeling it, let it come out! The more emotion and enthusiasm you put into the statements, the better.

When listening to your vision script, it can be helpful to get into a deeply relaxed state. At that level, your conscious mind is out of the way and it makes it easier to input the new information. Since I tend to fall asleep anyway, I play my vision script recording at bedtime. I follow along for a while and then leave it to my subconscious to do the rest of the work. I even add in statements early in the script to help facilitate that process. I also add statements about how I'll feel when I wake up—refreshed, energized, rejuvenated, excited and motivated, and most especially, knowing what I need to do and getting to it.

The sample script in the Transformation Insight below includes most of these suggestions. You don't have to use everything in it— or even anything—just use what works for you. Create a script that makes your dreams come alive and read it to yourself—or play your recording—daily. You'll be amazed how fast your thinking starts to shift!

The Written Version

If you're going to use your written script to read from each day, you will only use the main section of the sample script to create it. Disregard the opening relaxation statements and the closing section—you only need those for the recorded version.

Print out several copies of your script and keep them where you will see them. Keep one copy with your vision board. Read your statements either before or after you "live" your vision board—which ever feels most inspiring to you. Whenever you feel like you need a boost, you can always grab your script and read a few statements. The good feelings will come and you'll be inspired, motivated and back on track to making your dreams come true.

The Recorded Version

In order to create a recorded vision script, you obviously have to have a written one. You'll use the full example in the sample script below—modified to fit your needs—to create the script that you will read from to record. You can certainly read from it daily too—the more the merrier—but read aloud from just the main section, as explained above.

To create my vision scripts, I use a small digital recorder that I purchased for about $70. There are probably better ones now for less. You can also use cassette tapes—yes, some people still love them—or record on your computer and make a CD. Use your iPod, smartphone or any of a zillion other devices available.

However, be sure that you can be selective about what you play if you're going to fall asleep—you don't want to play your entire music library or other audio files to your subconscious mind. You want to be very clear about what you're inputting and why. What you say to yourself counts—even in music—so when you're working with your vision script, be sure that's all you're working with.

When recording your script, I highly recommend you make many smaller files rather than trying to record everything at one time. I usually put one to ten statements on a file so if I make a mistake or want to change something later, I don't have to redo the entire script—only a few statements. My recorder has several folders, so putting different types of statements in different folders makes it easier to add things in the correct section more easily.

I generally record the opening relaxation and closing sections separately and put them in the first and last folders, then spread the main section statements across the others. The sample script breaks things down into categories, such as general life, relationships, health, business and so on, so it's easy to separate for initial recording and then add to the sections as needed. Never hurts to drag a backup copy over to your computer either.

Technicalities

When I develop and record personalized vision scripts for clients, the entire script is in second person, using *you* and *your* rather than *I* and *my*. That makes sense because it's my voice and I'm talking to them. However, I do the same for the opening and closing sections of my own personal recordings. It just feels better to me to do that, because having a "guide" helps me relax and move into that deeper state more quickly. Then, once the guide has helped me relax, I switch to first person and use "I" statements. The sample vision script is structured in that way; however, if you prefer to use *I* for the entire script, that's fine. Or, if it feels better to use *you* throughout the whole thing, do that. Just do what feels comfortable for you and don't worry— your subconscious will get the message. If you already have a guided relaxation script that you like or a personal method that you use to get into that deeper state, use that for your introductory section. You know you and what works!

The sample script is based on our window-washer friend again— things I imagined him aspiring to. As you read through it, notice how it uses the words and phrases from his example answers to his Dream Distiller questions. Use the Dream Distiller to help you define the details for your own personalized statements. Go through the process for each thing you want to have in your life and develop statements accordingly.

The sample includes some general life, relationship and health statements to give you an idea about those as well. You can also get many more ideas on health and related statements from Louise Hay's book *You Can Heal Your Life* and other sources. Remember, the more specific the statements are to you and your way of thinking, the better the script will work for you.

Well, let's get to it! It's time to get clear on what living the life you love really means to you!

Create your vision script using the sample below, which uses our window-washer friend and his goals as examples.

Read or listen to your vision script daily—or both. Record your script and listen with stereo headphones when you want to relax or as you go to sleep. Listening to your own voice is a very effective method of getting through the conscious clutter and making significant mental shifts quickly. As I mentioned earlier, some mental dissonance—feeling a little "off"—is normal at first as your mind tries to reconcile the different versions of reality you're inputting. It should pass fairly quickly. If it doesn't, look over your statements and see if some might need rewording. I've never found anyone who couldn't work with positive affirming statements, but, as with everything, if it doesn't feel right, don't do it.

Note: I have put many different types of statements and examples in here so you can find what fits best for you—it's an extensive script. Read every statement and pick out the phrasing that fits and makes sense to you.

To save space, I've combined four or five sentences into one paragraph. When you draft your own script, it will be easier to read and record if you only put one thought per line and space things out more. Adapt, expand and customize!

Sample Vision Script

OPENING—Guided Relaxation Statements: Now it is time to relax. It's time to let go of all worries and concerns and just take a few moments for yourself to relax and let go. So, take a moment now and get very comfortable so that you can completely relax. You may want to move around a little bit or adjust your pillow or blanket—whatever you need to do to feel completely comfortable.

Now close your eyes. Because when you close your eyes, you find it even easier to relax. You may also want to take a deep breath, because when you take in a deep breath, it sends wonderful, relaxing and rejuvenating oxygen throughout your entire body. As you exhale, you feel that wonderful release as all tension and tightness flows gently and easily out of your body. You feel completely relaxed and comfortable from the top of your head all the way down through the tips of your toes. And remember, if you hear any sounds inside the room or outside the room, they are just normal background noise, and they will allow you to relax even further. This is your time, a time just for you.

This is a time to allow your mind to open to all the positive and beneficial statements that you have created for yourself, statements that describe the life you have always dreamed of living, the life that is now yours. And because you understand that what you think about becomes true for you, it is always easy to keep your thoughts on the wonderful things in your new life. It is easy to see and feel your new life, to feel the joy of living the life you love.

Now, because you are so very relaxed, it is easy for you to allow your conscious mind to relax and move into the background and to allow these wonderful, positive statements to go directly to the deepest part of your mind, where you can work with them in the most positive and helpful ways possible. Remember, this is your life and you are always in control. And as you relax even further, you feel more and more at peace, knowing that you are the authority in your life, feeling secure in your ability to make good choices, feeling strong and confident because you joyfully accept full responsibility for yourself and your life.

The following statements are messages from you to you. All are for your highest and greatest good and greatest joy, and they will be integrated into your consciousness on all levels to use in the most effective and helpful ways possible.

MAIN—Life Vision Statements

General: Yes! Just as I knew it would, taking control of my thoughts and my mind, and making positive and fulfilling choices, has created this incredibly amazing life I now live! I claimed my dreams and now I'm living them! I am happier than I have ever been. I wake up every day with a smile on my face, because I am truly living the life of my dreams and it is better than I even imagined! And how easy it is to keep creating my ideal world—I just see it and feel it and then I'm living it! I am so happy and having so much fun, I can hardly believe it. I love my life!

What fun it is to live my life! I am the best I've ever been! Yes, I *am* living my highest potential, and I'm loving every minute of it! I embrace change and know that only good is flowing into my life at all times! I am totally and completely at peace with my prosperity, my success, my joy, my happiness and my abundance. I am so grateful that I finally allowed myself to claim my dreams—that I am finally living the life I truly love. My life is filled with love, joy, happiness, fun, laughter, perfect health and prosperity. I love my life!

Business and Money: The transition to having my own window-washing business was so easy! And now I love washing windows even more than before, because it is my own business and I call the shots. Yes, I *am* in charge of my destiny, and I feel even more free and excited than I ever imagined. Yes, I took a big step, and it has turned out even better than I dreamed it would. Everything just fell into place! I did what I needed to do and it just always seemed that I was in the right place at the right time—I still am! I'm in alignment with my dreams and my world, and everything I need comes to me in the perfect way and time—always.

I already have a full schedule of the very best clients, and I'm getting more long-term contracts every day! My business is expanding and growing at an amazing, yet manageable and effective, rate. I always attract only the most skilled, capable, safe, responsible, honest and hard-working people to work with me, and I have a great team. Everyone gets along and supports one another. They love their jobs, do great work and have fun too! I knew it could be this way—and it is! I appreciate my fantastic employees and they are always telling me how much they appreciate me too, because of the safe, fair and fun work environment I provide. It makes me feel so good to be able to provide that for them. It's deeply fulfilling to know that I make a positive difference in others' lives. My customers love the great work my team and I do, and they enthusiastically recommend my company to others.

And really, what an amazing job I have! I love the feel of the breeze blowing across my face as I glide down the ropes with my crew, cleaning the glass, seeing the ocean and feeling salty air. I can't keep from smiling. I love my work! I love my life! I am so proud of myself for taking the chance and starting this business. I wanted it so badly I could taste it, and I knew if I put in the time and effort, it would be a success. And it is! I've done it! I still can't believe how I made it happen so easily and in the ways I wanted it to financially. The money and financing worked out even better than I had planned, and my income just keeps increasing every month. I'm already paying myself twice what I was making before! Yes, I've done it! I'm living my loftiest and happiest dreams on all levels. I have created my own abundant life and it has given me a sense of self, a true freedom and joy. I am living life to the fullest, and my life just keeps getting better and better every day!

Money is a tool that works for me and I appreciate it! It is such a relief to be free of financial worry—to easily be able to buy whatever I want or need! I love looking at my bank statements and seeing how much money I am earning. It feels good and I deserve it! My investments always pay off well for me! I always make great decisions and things always work out for my highest and greatest good. My dealings are always fair and work out for the highest good of all concerned. They are always win-win situations, and everyone gets a good deal and is happy for the way the situation resolves. And it always turns out that I have gotten great deals! I always make great decisions and things always work out for my highest and greatest good. I am totally and completely at peace with my prosperity, joy, happiness and abundance!

Relationships, Family and Home: I have only healthy relationships that bring me joy. I attract only positive, good, kind, honorable, supportive, responsible and like-minded people to me. The people in my life are positive and interesting, and our interactions are always mutually supportive, uplifting and mutually beneficial. I have an amazing network of friends and associates and some really wonderful close friends. I feel so blessed!

I live fully in the moment, in complete joy and without reservation or hesitation, because I trust that all who now come into my life bring only joy. I live and breathe healthy behaviors. I am so at peace since I found my own self-respect and started valuing myself. It changed everything! I see things so differently now that I love and respect myself. Everything makes sense and it's so easy to make wise choices. I do my best every day and am always looking for ways to be even better. I find myself smiling and laughing all the time. I completely and totally enjoy every moment. I love my new life and the people in it!

Even though I wasn't really looking, I found the love of my life! It is so amazing how much we have in common, how we value and appreciate the same things and how well we get along. We both love to travel and she loves animals just as much as I do! It's so easy being with her! I feel happy, excited, and calm and peaceful all at the same time. It's amazing! It's so easy to be myself and to be honest. We're best friends and so much more. It feels amazing—and real, better than anything I've ever experienced before. We're even talking about starting a family! Me! It's so amazing! I love the changes in my life—and in me. I love me!

And my new home! I love it! As with everything else, things just fell into place easily and naturally. My house sold quickly, and since things were already going so well with the business, I was able to buy another one—my dream home! The timing worked out perfectly and so did the money! I got top dollar for my old home and found a good deal on my new one with a willing and grateful seller. Everything was so easy. My dealings are always fair and work out for the highest and greatest good of all concerned. They are always win-win situations, and everyone gets a good deal and is happy for the way the situation resolves.

Health: I love how great I look and feel! I am stronger, healthier and more energized than I ever have been. I am passionate about healthy eating and healthy habits. I am fully in tune with my body, and I always intuitively know what it needs. I have perfect, vibrant health, and I feel wonderful! My body is working absolutely perfectly, and I am amazed at how fit and strong I am — and how great I feel!

I always make healthy choices in foods, drinks and activities, and I give my body the very best of what it needs to maintain optimal health and fitness. It is so easy is to get the exercise my body needs—and I love doing it! I now automatically choose what is best for me and for my body. I love how great my body feels when I make healthy choices! It makes it so easy to make more healthy choices! I wake up every day, feeling great, always full of energy, happiness and a positive attitude. I am so deeply grateful for this wonderful body I have that takes such good care of me, and I'm so glad I take such good care of it too! I am so grateful for the amazing life I now live. I love my life. I love my body. I love me!

CLOSING—Guided Session Closure: Now it's time to allow these wonderful, uplifting, inspiring and empowering messages to flow through you, to be you. These statements, thoughts, images and words are yours, just as are the things and situations they describe—the life they describe, your life. Allow yourself to continue to experience the positive feelings these words bring you. Feel the happiness and joy of living the life you have always wanted, because you *are* living it. It's yours.

You easily remember the words and messages in this recording, and they remind you of how amazing and wonderful your life is now. And the more you listen, the more joy, fun and happiness you have. You find yourself constantly noticing things that put you closer to your goals, and you automatically feel the same wonderful feelings of success and accomplishment as you do here, which inspires you even more.

When it is time for you to get up, you will wake up automatically at the desired time, feeling absolutely wonderful. You will wake up feeling refreshed, rejuvenated, in complete balance, full of joy and totally energized, ready to enjoy every moment of your day. Remember, you easily and automatically awaken at the exact time you need to, feeling absolutely wonderful, refreshed and rejuvenated and full of energy and joy!

CHAPTER 24

33 TIPS FOR THE DIPS

If you don't like the way things are, complaining
isn't going to fix anything—doing is.

Well, you've done it! You know what you want, you've run your dreams through the Dream Distiller, you've made your vision board and vision script. Now you're set and everything will be perfect from here on out!

Well, probably not. Life is about peaks and valleys. The great news is that once you've learned to look at yourself and the world differently—as I hope you've done with this book—the peaks just get better and better, and the valleys become just little dips that remind you how great the peaks are. Still, no matter how great things are, when you do hit a dip, it can catch you off guard.

Have you ever had one of those days when you just went blank? You didn't see it coming, but one day, there it was. You woke up in a fog and everything seemed out of whack, and for the life of you, you couldn't think of a single positive, motivating or inspiring thing to do to pull yourself out of the funk. It happens.

If you hit a bump in the road or a dip in your trip, find yourself treading water with no shoreline in sight or just need a reminder of what you already know to do, here are a few things that might help move you back onto solid ground. Here's a list of things to do when you don't know what to do.

1. Throw a Pity Party

Yes, really. If you find yourself in the midst of a gnarly ball of self-pity, go for it. It beats trying to keep that horrible feeling at bay for days on end, pretending you aren't angry or don't want to bawl your eyes out, so do it and get it out. Set a timer for ten minutes and rant and rave, wallow and wail, moan and groan, punch a pillow or just plain sob. Then, when the timer buzzes, you're done. You'll feel better and can get on with your life. The more you allow yourself to own your feelings—instead of fighting to pretend you don't have them—the sooner you'll resolve them.

2. Lighten Up

Obviously, after the pity party's over, you'll need to find something else to do. When you're ready to crawl out of the abyss and into the light, find something positive, uplifting, inspiring or motivational, or something that simply makes you laugh. It doesn't have to be some deeply spiritual material. In some of my darker moments, my favorite authors just didn't speak to me. I didn't feel very spiritual and I sure wasn't interested in delving into any more of my own "issues" or trying to talk myself out of my feelings. Somehow, I stumbled across Bob Parsons's video blogs on godaddy.com, which are half pep talk and half standup routine. Such as they are, they were just what I needed. I laughed—and I paid attention to what he said. Success speaks! Before long, I was back on track and moving forward again.

We need different things at different times. Give yourself permission to get what you need, even if it seems a bit out of character for you. And laugh!

3. Do Nothing

That's right—do absolutely *nothing*. If you don't want to cry—or laugh—maybe it's time to just veg out. We're wired to feel guilty about it, but taking some time off and curling up with a good book, having a movie marathon day or just lounging around in pajamas can be really good for us. We can't fly high all the time, and taking a break from our fast-paced lives to refuel and do a little internal maintenance can keep us from falling off our hamster wheels in exhaustion—or combustion.

Oftentimes, the dip doesn't last long, and we pop back into gear and become our cheery selves once again. And sometimes just telling ourselves that it's okay to have flat days makes the downtime shorter. We come out of it quicker, because there's no internal pressure telling us that we're doing something wrong by not being "up" all the time. Choosing to take it easy for a day is far better than having a health issue force you into it. So, if you're just not feeling it, embrace the moment and do whatever you want to—or nothing at all. It may be exactly what you need.

4. Plot a Murder

No, not a *real* murder. As you may know, I write humorous mystery novels too, and, believe it or not, *those* were *my* therapy books—not this one. There's something cathartic about having the power to go back and wreak havoc in ways you couldn't at the time. In fiction, you're in control and you can write your story any way you want to. Anyone who ever wronged you can very simply—and perhaps gruesomely— die! At least that was my plan when I wrote those first books. As it turned out, however, once I started writing and worked through my issues with the people, I didn't feel like killing them anymore—and I was having a lot of fun writing as well. So, if you've got a story to tell or an axe to grind, sit down at the keyboard and start writing. You might feel a whole lot better, and who knows, you might even get a publishable book out of the deal.

5. Seek Counsel

After the last suggestion, this one is probably appropriate. If you really do have a lot of anger, grief, anxiety or other unresolved emotional issues, get some help with them. Sometimes we don't have a realistic view of what we're saying and doing—or why. Whether it's a health crisis, a painful relationship or a career collapse, we can become so focused on avoiding those pesky trees that we have no concept of the forest we're lost in. That's where an objective observer can be very helpful. Some best friends, and even some mates, can put their own vested interests and personal desires aside and give you sound feedback, but when you're trying to find your way out of a dark forest, it's generally better to have a park ranger at your side. Someone who's seen you bash your head into the same tree forty-two times might not even notice it anymore, whereas the park ranger would see it instantly. Also, you won't have to worry that you're being steered in a particular direction because a professional counselor won't have a personal interest in your choices and decisions.

If you want help figuring out a direction or setting goals and mapping out a plan to achieve them, a qualified coach can help. If you're ready to tackle the deep stuff, find a qualified professional therapist or counselor who can listen to what you're saying and reflect it back to you honestly, without a personal agenda—or social, familial or any other kind—coloring the process.

6. Dump Approval Ratings

Are you feeling bad because of what you think someone else thinks about you? Here's a phrase you may have heard before—memorize it: *"Your opinion of me is none of my business."*

"Wait," you say, "it is too my business and it does too matter!" Okay, why? If you're doing your very best and being the best person you can be, who really has the problem here? If you have to act in a certain way so someone will like or approve of you, well, guess what, they don't, won't and never will. Sure, if you learn to sit, stay and roll over the way they tell you to, you *might* be thrown a bone, but it's not about you. It can't be, because those tricks aren't really who you are. So, let go of the need to have approval from anyone. Yes, your parents, your mate, your best friends and even your boss. Sure, you have to do your job and be a decent human being, but you don't have to be a suck-up. Stop worrying about whether people like you. Focus on doing what's right because it is the right thing to do, and the reward will be that you like yourself!

7. Take Out the Trash

When I get in a rut, generally, so does my house—I let things go. I put off dealing with my own junk—literally and figuratively—and things start to pile up. Sometimes, simply cleaning up my mess on the outside helps me out of my mess on the inside. With things cleared out and cleaned up, I feel better, and my view of the world may even be different. Something as simple as cleaning off your desk or countertop can help. So, if you're stuck, take out the trash and free up some space—physical and mental.

8. Feng Shui It

Ever heard of Feng Shui? It's the Chinese art of arranging things—furniture, plants, water, decorations—to create a positive flow of energy. One of the first steps is decluttering, so after you've taken out the trash, see if there's more you can do to stir up some good vibes. Find a book that makes it simple and try some of the techniques. A plant can bring a touch of color, lively energy and oxygen. Add a fountain and relax to the sounds of trickling water. Just doing a few things could change the feel of your space and bring peace, tranquility or even creativity into areas of your life where you need it.

9. Change the Channel

Do I really have to tell you that if you feel bad after watching or listening to something, you need to stop doing it? Well, I'm going to, because I am continually amazed at how people think it doesn't matter—it does. If you put it into your brain, it has an effect—period. So, for one week, stop watching anything that causes you anxiety or makes you feel bad. Whether it's the news, a crime-solvers drama or some reality show, if it's immersing you in the dark side of human nature, *stop watching it.* How can you expect to be cheerful and happy when you're constantly bombarding your senses and emotions with murder, mayhem, drama and fear?

I just watched *Angels and Demons* again a few days ago. The portrayal of the media reporting the "news" is excellent. What's going out as news and what's actually happening are two wildly different stories. It's true in real life too. So, if you know you're rarely hearing the authentic story, why expose yourself and your blood pressure to it? I'm not saying be blind to what's going on in the world, but unless your job requires it, you really don't need to know how horrible things are every moment of the day.

As for the drama and crime shows you like to watch, record them if you must, but wait at least a week before you even consider looking at them. Just for a week, keep your focus on things you have control over, such as working toward your goals, maintaining a positive frame of mind, doing things that make you smile and laugh, and feeling good. Think about what's right in the world. After you've been away from the drama drain for a while you'll know what you want to allow back into your world, what you can tolerate while staying positive and what you no longer need.

Surround yourself with positive programming instead. Watch, listen to and read things that make you feel good, because when you feel good, you spread the good around. Just like little butterfly wings, your positive energy ripples throughout your world and does more good than you can possibly know. Good stuff in, good stuff out and more good stuff coming back to you!

10. Color Outside the Lines

Do something different—anything! Break your routines. Start noticing what you do—what you do automatically without thinking about it—

and see how you might do it differently. Hold your coffee cup with your opposite hand, take a different route to work, walk a different path to the copy machine, try an exotic restaurant, order chicken instead of beef. You could buy a red shirt instead of your regular beige or wear your watch on your other arm. Instead of automatically turning on the TV when you walk in the door, you could listen to music, enjoy the quiet or maybe change clothes and go for a walk—anything that tells your inner self you're willing to do things differently. Making simple shifts to routines on purpose paves the way for making other changes. Once your mind realizes it's no big deal to do things differently, you'll have less resistance when you want to make bigger moves.

11. Learn Mind Control

Yes, it would be dandy if you could control someone else's mind, but this is about controlling yours. Unless you've worked at managing your thoughts on purpose, you don't really have much control over what you think. Go ahead and give it a try. Focus your mind on only one thought—let's use purple pigs—and see how long you can keep your thoughts only on that. The second another thought slips in, such as "This is really stupid" or "Why not pink rabbits?", you'll see what I mean. It's much harder than you'd think it would be—at least it is for me.

Actually, the mind is just doing its job—thinking—and unless we're actively at the controls, it goes where it wants. Being able to keep your mind focused on what *you* want it focused on, rather than whatever comes up in the queue, is an important skill. It comes in particularly handy when you get something stuck in your head and want it out, such as an annoying song, or perhaps an obsessive thought about a boyfriend or something else you have no control over.

Here's a good exercise to start negotiating with your mind on who's calling the shots in your head. Sit in a straight-backed chair at a table—quietly, of course—with an object on it a few feet in front of you. The object can be anything—a candle, an ink pen, a piece of jewelry, a crystal, a coffee cup, anything that you can direct your mind to focus on for a few minutes. Sit upright with your feet on the floor, your spine straight and your hands in your lap. Focus on the object and only the object. Keep your thoughts directed to exploring every aspect of it, the way it shines, its shape, its texture, its color, what it's made of, how it's put together. When an unrelated thought comes in, simply let it go and bring your focus back to exploring the object.

This is good practice for meditation, and indeed it *is* meditation—a mindful, deliberate focus. You may have heard people suggest you let your mind go blank. Well, it's a nice thought, but if you could do it, how would you know? This is simply about learning to use what you have more effectively. So, set a timer and do the above exercise for three minutes. Work your way up to five minutes, then seven, then ten. This trains the mind to accept your control and to stay focused on one thing without going off on a tangent, as it normally does.

12. Spelunk the Cranial Cave

We're still going mental, but this is different from mind control or plain downtime where you just hang out and don't think. This is about cutting out all the distractions and diversions and finding out what's stirring around in your cranium—and why. It's about discovering what you'd be thinking about if you weren't parked in front of the TV, talking on the phone or frittering away time on the Internet.

Some people can't be alone without having some kind of noise for company. They keep the TV going constantly to fill the silence. It may make them feel like they're not alone or keep them distracted from thoughts they'd rather not think—or both. Sometimes, however, thinking is exactly what you need to do. If you've been using distractions, diversions and even dramas to avoid thinking about things, now's the time to suck it up, get your flashlight and go exploring.

Find a quiet place, and with pen and paper in hand—or fingers on the keyboard—sit comfortably and just let your mind wander. Don't try to direct your thoughts as you do in the mind-control exercise—just notice what comes up and write it down. If something pops up you want to explore further, go with it. Make notes about everything and see where it takes you. Spend at least ten minutes. The point is to discover what your mind wants to talk to you about so you can make peace with it. You have a book full of discovery tools in your hands, so as the important stuff reveals itself, run it through an appropriate Transformation Insight. And, as always, if there's an issue you need professional help with, get it.

13. Learn Something

Be a lifelong learner. Formally or informally, keep yourself learning things. Take a class on something that interests you, attend a motivational conference, go on a retreat or go to a museum. There are so many amazing and fun things to do and ways to do something on any budget. Not only does it keep you from appearing brain dead, you'll also discover people, places, things and activities in your own hometown that you never knew about. You'll have new experiences, meet new people and start seeing the world from a bigger perspective. Besides, people who've educated themselves on a wide variety of topics, and are passionate about learning and life, are much more fun and interesting to be around.

14. Play the "What If?" Game

If you could have, be or do anything you wanted, what would it be? Forget about all the reasons it's not possible and just focus on what you want. Play out the dream with no restrictions. Get the image clear and real in your head. Do this as often as you like. It is fun to "try on" new places to live, new jobs, new cars and so on. Some may just be entertaining distractions that you really don't want to pursue. Others may inspire you to make them a part of your life. Try it! *"What if I . . ."*

15. Take a Hike

Getting out and walking in nature is not only good for getting the body moving and getting healthy, it's also great for relaxing and releasing stress. Getting out in this amazing world we live in and really being in it—seeing it, hearing it, smelling it and feeling it—puts a lot of things in perspective. Maybe it's partly to do with that natural negative-ion-balancing thing that's always going on, but being out in nature is a natural stress buster. Want to expand your view of the natural world even more? Take Stephen Skinner's *Sacred Geometry* with you on your next trek and discover nature's divinely ordered and mathematically definable fractal patterns. Once you start seeing them, you'll never look at things the same away again. There are all kinds of interesting ways to appreciate the beauty of this incredible planet!

16. Play with Rocks

Nature *is* absolutely fascinating, so dig into a specific area that interests you, such as birds, bugs or fish. Discover the wildflowers common to your area and learn what plants are edible. Become a rock hound and go hunting for special stones. Learn their properties and what they've been used for throughout history. *The Encyclopedia of Crystals* by Judy Hall has beautiful pictures and gives all kinds of diverse information—types of crystalline structures, hardness factors, metaphysical properties and uses by ancient cultures. Explore, expand and enjoy!

17. Give Back

Get outside of yourself and do something to help someone else. It could be an elderly neighbor, a family that's struggling or someone who's just having a bad day. If you see something that needs to be done, do it. If there's a need, fill it—preferably in such a way that no one else knows you did it. This *doesn't* mean finding someone you think needs fixing so you can focus on her life instead of yours.

Contact a local organization in your community and volunteer. If they don't need hands-on help, ask what's on their wish list—what do they need to keep the doors open—or ask what someone they're working with may need, then take care of it.

18. Accept Gifts

It's great to give, and some of us are really good at that, but not so good at receiving. Allow others to give to you for a change. Giving and doing for others may be second nature, but you have to get comfortable with letting others do for you too. Allow yourself to be nurtured for a little while. You can go back to being the giver tomorrow. And remember, it makes you feel good to give, so don't deprive others of feeling good when they want to give to you.

19. Delve into Your Dreams

We spend a third of our life asleep, and a lot of mental processing goes on during that time. The mind uses symbols to relay information, and sometimes what we consider nightmares are simply the mind's way of getting our attention so that we'll remember. This is a great way to get some insight on what's really going on beneath the conscious awareness, what's really at the root of your situation, your concerns and your fears.

Many books explore dream interpretation. My favorite is *The Dream Book: Symbols for Self-Understanding* by the late Betty Bethards. The first half of the book gives a great explanation of the types of dreams we have—information processing, junk clearing, message dreams and others. The second half is a dictionary of symbols and basic interpretations. I love this book and it's helped me get a lot of insight when I really needed it. I couldn't hide from my issues, even in my dreams.

20. Be an Alien Observer

Imagine you just arrived on this planet and don't know anything about it. What do you see? How do you interpret it? Step back and take on the role of an objective observer. Put away the filter of your own experiences, beliefs and prejudices and look at the world as though you've never seen it before. Be willing to see the faults of the people, groups and ideals you identify with—and to see the good in those you don't. You might just come away from the experience with a better view of the world—and yourself.

21. Do an Exposure Inventory

Who do you spend the most time with? What do you do? How do you feel when you're with them? How do you feel afterward? Do you have to be with these people or are you choosing to? Since you already know you become who your friends are, choose wisely and hang around with people who are doing good things and cultivating positive energy. Surround yourself with positive people and feel your world start to get lighter. You can't stay negative around positive people, because they won't allow it. Either you come to the positive side, or they won't hang around with *you*.

22. Do a Time Inventory

Take inventory of how you spend your time. How much time do you spend in front of the TV? How much time reading, exercising, eating, sleeping, working, learning? What do you do for fun? What do you do because you have to? What do you do because you choose to? How much of it brings you joy? What makes you feel nurtured? What feels like punishment? Asking yourself these things periodically can help you stay aware of whether your life is in balance and whether you're doing things because you want to or because you think you have to.

23. Be Grateful

Gratitude refocuses your attention on what's working in your life rather than what isn't, and that automatically shifts you from feeling bad to feeling good. Be grateful and thankful for everything you have right now, even if it isn't exactly what you want. Being thankful opens the door for even better things. You can even be grateful for experiences that weren't all that great, because they served important purposes in your life. Things that seem "bad" when they happen are sometimes great gifts when we look back on them. So, appreciate all your experiences!

24. Spruce Yourself Up

Sometimes we can get into a rut, and a new style on the outside can help reflect the changes taking place on the inside. It can be a new shirt, a new hairstyle or simply "dressing up." Find something in your closet that you'd wear to a job interview, on a first date or to a special event. Put it on, fix your hair, polish your shoes—do your thing, head to toe, to make sure you look your best. You can go to work like this, or out with friends, to the grocery store, to the mall or to lunch by yourself. Whatever you do, if you go out looking good, you'll automatically feel good—inside and out.

25. Find Some Good Vibes

Put on music that you would listen to if you were setting out on a road trip. You know, the tunes that make you want to turn up the volume and sing along. Play something that always makes you feel good. I've been on a classic-rock kick lately, and some of those old songs from back when trigger good feelings for me and can help get me in a better place. It's hard to stay in a funk when a favorite tune is rocking out an upbeat tempo.

26. Get a Massage

Oh, yeah, twice even. Some people get squeamish about even saying the word—*massage*—and I used to be one of them. But once you get over the idea that there's anything sexual about a massage, you'll be hauling yourself to the spa every chance you get. All massages are not created equal, however, nor are all massage therapists. Most states have licensing requirements, so be sure you're working with a pro. And, of course, check with your physician if you have any special health issues to take into consideration.

Try a few different therapists until you find the technique and style that suits you best. A relaxing massage is different from a deep-tissue or a therapeutic massage. If you want the kinks worked out, say so, but if you only want to be pampered, then request that. Many massages incorporate essential oils, which are wonderful. They smell good and they have their own therapeutic properties as well. You can also add hot stones, a facial, reflexology—a special technique for massaging the acupressure points on the feet—or a host of other specialty services. Do a little research and give it a try. You might find out you like it—a lot!

27. Make a List

Call it a Bucket List if you must, but make it. List all the things you've always wanted to do or think you might want to do. Then jot down why you think you'd like to do them. What do you think the experience will be like? How do you think you'll feel when you're doing these things? Is there any one of those things that you could do now? Or soon? Making a list starts making possibilities real. By saying you want to do something, writing it down and thinking about how much fun it would be if you did, you get on your way to actually doing it. We're all dying, so don't wait until your expiration date is staring you in the face. Make that list now and start doing!

28. Try Yoga, Tai Chi, Qigong

Yoga classes are a good way to connect the mind and body and cultivate inner calmness and peace—not to mention help with balance and give your muscles a workout. They're also a whole lot harder than they look. To watch, it can seem like there's not much of anything going on. Well, let me assure you that there is. I've been in plenty of those nothing-looking yoga poses, trying to focus on my breath instead of the fact that my muscles were quivering and I was about to die. It's not like pumping iron or running a marathon, but it's a workout—for body and mind. Tai chi and qigong are about aligning breath and movement and offer similar benefits with their own approaches. Qigong, however, can also fall into the next item on this list, which is moving energy. These things aren't the latest fitness craze—body-mind-breath training has been around for centuries—so visit a class and see what you think.

29. Learn Energy Work

What I call "energy work" is simply focusing the energy that's all around us every day and directing it for healing wherever it's needed. It's a little like those physical-therapy devices that use small electric charges to stimulate muscles to contract. A battery holds the energy and the device delivers it to the area that needs to be stimulated, only in this case *you* are the device directing the energy. It feels good and is very relaxing, and it's something you can do for anyone or for yourself.

Years ago—a lot of years—my best friend nagged me to go with her to a Reiki Level I training class. I thought she was not right in the head and told her so. Well, after my divorce, my whole outlook changed and I started exploring all kinds of different things. I wound up in a Reiki class on a lark, but once the class got going, I knew I'd be learning everything I could about energy work. Quantum-Touch, Healing Touch and Therapeutic Touch are other techniques that basically do the same type of thing—channel energy for healing. It's about focus, resonance and entrainment, and anyone can do it, whether you understand the technicalities or not. And, if everyone *would* do it, the world would certainly be a different place, because we'd all be focused on how we could *help* each other.

Many Western medicine professionals now incorporate energetic healing and other modalities into their practices, as do many hospitals. It's also a routine part of some cancer treatment programs, and some schools require it for students training to become registered nurses. Some physicians are still skeptical of—and opposed to—anything other than traditional Western allopathic medicine, but the tide has turned, and more and more are realizing the benefits of incorporating other techniques. The stories about that in the section below may surprise you, so read on.

30. Go Unconventional and Traditional

A couple of years ago, I sat by a young woman on a plane who was a medical student from Arizona. I was so excited! I had a future doctor captive, and I was going to use the flight time to convince her to include alternative techniques in her practice. Well, it turned out she was way ahead of me. She was in the integrative-medicine program that Dr. Andrew Weil started a couple of decades ago at the University of Arizona. I didn't have to convince her of *anything*. She and her sister, who was a naturopathic physician (ND) and also certified in a long list of alternative therapeutic techniques, were going into practice together, incorporating conventional Western medicine with traditional Eastern medicine and everything in between. What a thrill it was to hear her talk about what she was doing! The medical world *is* adapting and things *are* changing, which is good for everyone.

Mental-health professionals have also embraced new ways of thinking. Some techniques that have been around for a long time, such as hypnosis, are now being used in different ways, and new methods that work with energetic pathways (meridians) and acupressure points to facilitate psychological healing are also in widespread use. The field of Energy Psychology encompasses a wide area of methods and techniques, such as EFT (Emotional Freedom Technique, also known as tapping) and EMDR (Eye Movement Desensitization and Reprocessing). Whatever the approach, the goal is to utilize the body's own energetic workings to interrupt patterns, discharge intense emotional reactions, help people deal with traumas, and treat post-traumatic stress disorder and other conditions. There are *many* options for getting help today—traditional, conventional, unconventional, alternative, and any combination thereof. Some additional healing modalities include acupuncture, acupressure, aromatherapy, sound, light and other wave therapies, biofeedback methods, regression, dream interpretation and health intuitive readings, to name a very few.

We all need different things at different times, and exploring something off your beaten path may be worth considering. Some people find insight through guided and individual spiritual experiences based on Native American or Eastern cultural rituals. Some seek the assistance of an intuitive reader, spiritual medium, astrologist, shaman or any of a wide variety of healers and practitioners for guidance, insight and healing—but remember, others are only guides, and no one knows you better than *you*. There are many opportunities for learning and many ways to support the journey inward, so keep an open mind, but don't try anything that doesn't feel right to you. Explore what interests you, learn from many and embrace what helps you find your own way.

31. Make a Vision Board and Script

If you haven't made your vision board and vision script yet, flip back to Chapters 22 and 23 and make them. To recap, a vision board is simply a board, paper or digital file showing images of you with things you want in your life, along with inspiring quotes and other relevant statements. Put in the picture of your perfect house, photos of places you want to travel or the car you want to drive, as well as images that evoke feelings, such as two people walking hand in hand for love, a spa scene for pampering, babies and children for family—you get the idea. Put the board where you can see it every day and spend a few minutes imagining yourself living it. Same for your vision script. Write and record positive and emotion-filled statements that describe your new life as if you're already living it. Put feeling into it—get excited about how great it is to live your new life. Read the written version and/or listen to your recorded audio version daily.

32. Be the Change

If you don't like the way things are, complaining isn't going to fix anything—doing is. Remember, just because someone throws you a ball doesn't mean you have to catch it. If you don't want to keep replaying the same old dramas or continue to feel taken advantage of or disrespected, well, stop allowing it—stop catching the ball—change the pattern. Be the person you think everyone else should be. If your focus is on being the best *you* and doing *your* very best in every situation, everything else will fall into place—even if the ball-throwers find someone else to play catch with. The changes will be good ones, and your world will automatically align to meet your new attitude. To paraphrase Gandhi, *be the change you want to see.*

33. Own Your Power

Your life is your responsibility, no one else's. There's only one thing standing between you and your dreams and that's you. Be open to new ideas and new options—you can't do what you've always done and expect anything to change in your life. It's also not up to anyone else to do anything for you. Being handed your dream life on a silver platter would be thrilling for a while, but then you'd be right back in the same boat, feeling something was missing and wanting more, because what you really needed couldn't be filled from the outside. When you accomplish things yourself, you feel empowered. You get the sense of accomplishment and pride that comes from doing—that wonderful feeling of "I did that!"

Always remember that *you* are the ultimate authority in your life. Don't give your power away to another person or group, or to an old negative pattern or limiting belief. If you don't like something, change it. What you think, say and do are up to you, so take responsibility for where you've been, where you are today—and where you're going tomorrow. Empower yourself by owning your right to choose and doing things on purpose.

TRANSFORMATION INSIGHT 24

List the ideas, tips or suggestions from this chapter that sound interesting and that you might like to explore. Note a situation where you think they might be helpful for quick reference, such as, "When I'm feeling _____, I could _____." Now start exploring.

Tip or idea	Notes
1.	
2.	
3.	
4.	

Tip or idea	Notes
5.	
6.	
7.	
8.	
9.	
10.	

CONCLUSION

Now that you've made it through the tunnel to the other side, take a moment and read through the letter from a best friend again.

Look, I know you're in pain and I hate seeing you hurt. I've tried everything I know to try to help you. I have listened and sympathized. I have offered suggestions and recommendations. I have sent you websites, books, CDs and movies to help get you through this. Nothing is working. So, because I care about you and I care about myself, I am going to tell you that you have to make a choice. You can choose to stay in pain if you want to. It's your life. But if you do, I will assume that your situation and your pain are what you want and I will honor your right to keep them. I will no longer make suggestions about things you can do to feel better, nor will I suggest that you change anything about your life. I will also no longer listen to you complain about your drama, because it serves no purpose. Either do what you need to do to change what you need to change, or admit that you don't want to and shut up about it.

How do you feel about it now? What thoughts came up this time as you read those tough words again? Were they different than they were before? Do you *feel* different? What's different in your life now? Big things? Little things? Do you talk about the same things? Think the same thoughts?

Probably not, because if you've read this book and worked through the Transformation Insights, you know a lot of things—powerful things. And once you know, you can never un-know and that's a really good thing.

Remember the equation for joy? Reality + Self-Respect + Action = Joy? Well, you're living it.

You can't hide behind your old mask of denial and delusion and pretend things are okay when they aren't. You can't pretend you're confused or don't know what to do anymore—you do. You know that you're going to do what someone with high self-esteem and self-respect would do—*every time*. The reality genie is not only out of the bottle, you've made friends with her and your Belief Monkey, and they now do your bidding.

Since you've taken personal responsibility for your life and owned your power of choice, you've probably noticed yourself smiling more, laughing more and feeling better. It's almost like magic! But it's even better than magic because it's real, and it doesn't take special tricks or illusions to pull it off. You no longer have to hide, lie or pretend to be someone you aren't—or try to be who someone else wants you to be. You're just being your fabulous authentic self, and somewhere along the road, you really started liking *you*!

The success stories I hear from you are absolutely amazing! How something as simple as asking yourself, "What are you willing to do?" and holding yourself accountable motivated you to do things you never thought you could—a new dream job, a seemingly impossible promotion, a new and healthy relationship, you name it. You became willing and your world changed. And when you share how you did what you never thought you could, and how it transformed you in the process, you positively glow. The joy, self-respect and pride radiated in your face and embodied in your words are unmistakable. You're happy!

Who knew it could be so easy? Okay, it wasn't easy at all, it was brutal—at least at first. But once you realized that letting the "bad" stuff up into the light wouldn't kill you, it got easier. You started reprogramming your limited thinking and put your Belief Monkey to work on the good stuff. You've made a huge difference in yourself and your own life, but you've also affected everyone else in your world, even me. Your transformation has shifted the dynamics in your world and sent that positive ripple out through the universe. By healing your life and doing things differently, you've set an example and you've given others the opportunity and inspiration to transform as well. Your joy has enriched us all, creating more joy. Thank you!

Keep living the life you love!

ADDITIONAL RESOURCES

There are many great books and audio and video presentations to choose from. The following is a quick alphabetical list of a few of my favorite authors, references from the text and other titles that you might find helpful. There are many programs and books out there, so find what speaks to you!

Richard Bach, *Illusions*; *Jonathan Livingston Seagull*

Melody Beattie, *Codependent No More*

Betty Bethards, *The Dream Book: Symbols for Self Understanding*

Rhonda Byrne, *The Secret*

Jack Canfield, *The Success Principles*

Steven Carter and Julia Sokol, *What Smart Women Know*

Cary Craig, *The Official EFT™ Tutorial*

Mike Dooley, *Infinite Possibilities*; *Leveraging the Universe*

Wayne Dyer, PhD, *Manifesting Your Destiny*; *The Power of Intention*

Louise Hay, *You Can Heal Your Life*; *You Can Heal Your Body*

Judy Hall, *The Encyclopedia of Crystals*

Harville Hendrix, PhD, *Getting the Love You Want*

Dr. Bernard Jensen, *Foods That Heal*

Anne Katherine, *Boundaries: Where You End and I Begin*

Caroline Myss, PhD, *Sacred Contracts*; *Self-Esteem*; *Why People Don't Heal*

Anthony Robbins, *The Ultimate Edge*

Don Miguel Ruiz, *The Four Agreements*; *The Mastery of Love*

Stephen Skinner, *Sacred Geometry*

Christopher Vogler, *The Writer's Journey*

Krystal Harpin

Paula Renaye is a five-time award-winning author, certified professional coach and transformational speaker. She is a frequent tough-love expert on talk radio shows and in print media, and her television appearances include BookTV. Writing as Paula Boyd, she and her award-winning Jolene Jackson Mystery Series have been featured in *Redbook, Mountain Living, San Antonio Woman, Romantic Times, Colorado Homes and Living* and many others. For more tips on how to live the life you love and to learn more about Paula Renaye and her work, visit www.paularenaye. com. To book Paula for a speaking engagement, seminar or motivational presentation, email paula@paularenaye.com.